FRIENDS
FIRST

An intuitive approach to <u>great</u> relationships!

Robert E. Hall

FRIENDS FIRST
an intuitive approach to great relationships

Visit www.friendsfirst.us or www.gudapublishing.com

Will love last longer if you are friends first? Dr. Grace Cornish, Jet magazine, Nov., 1999, copyright 1999 Johnson Publishing Co.

iUniverse books may be ordered through booksellers or by contacting:

iUniverse
1663 Liberty Drive
Bloomington, IN 47403
www.iuniverse.com
1-800-Authors (1-800-288-4677)

ISBN: 978-1-4620-2585-5 (sc)
ISBN: 978-1-4620-2586-2 (ebook)

Printed in the United States of America

iUniverse rev. date: 6/6/2011

友谊

Friendship

This book is dedicated to the wonderful loves of my life who have also remained my dearest friends,

to my beautiful and talented daughter Brittani,

to my siblings, Annie, Chris, and Chandler,

and, to my loving and tirelessly supportive parents Martha and Ted, who were friends first, and who continue to show their family what a relationship based on genuine friendship looks and feels like.

This book is also dedicated to my Uncle Jake.

The youngest son of Virginia and Harvey Daye, he was a strong, funny, and courageous man who lived his life authentically and who loved his family with his whole heart. Thank you for teaching the rest of us how to laugh at ourselves and with each other.

Contents

"All love that has not friendship for its base is like a mansion built upon the sand."

Ella Wheeler Wilcox

Acknowledgements

Introduction

The epiphany

The fourth step: On 'acquaintances'   58

Part III   The relationship 'cycle'

The fifth step: The relationship 'cycle'   70

Part IV   *You* and *Me* part 2

Part VI   *Your* relationship 'toolbox'

Acknowledgments

"If you want a friend, you have to be a friend."

Dale Carnegie

Books worthy of print are seldom the singular inspiration or the solitary scribing of an author. Such is the case with FRIENDS FIRST; a writing inspired by a daily *'man talk'* on relationships shared over the last decade with my friend and Radio colleague Kevin 'KJ' Johnson.

The thoughts, the statements of fact, the suggestions and the strategies contained in the pages that follow are the best representation of a philosophy evolved over the last thirty years regarding relationships. This book offers proverbial wisdoms that line up with what I, and - as it turns out – noted relationship specialists believe to be the healthiest and most productive methods of identifying and managing that part of the human condition – social relationships – too easily neglected.

It is my hope that FRIENDS FIRST offers *you* an easy and intuitive *who, how* and *why* approach to better managing *your* role as a real friend in thriving, challenging, newly formed, or future relationships.

I believe that each of us encounters wonderful earth-bound angels. They have loved, nurtured, supported, and - most importantly - forgiven my shortcomings as a relationship partner. I feel very fortunate to call my former relationship partners life-long friends and I cherish the gift of our enduring bonds.

Thank you Tom & Karen Haddaway. Your loving and unselfish relationship, your family, your honesty, and the unwavering friendship you have shown me have impacted my life and this writing beyond measure.

Thank you Tanya & Stafford Mack for sharing your courageous and honest journey as a couple and for never failing to remind me that we are indeed friends.

Thank you Dave Causey & Miriam Weaver. I admire your relationship and adore your candor and your shared joy for life. I consider you dear and precious friends.

Thank you Charlie & Christine Davis. I value our friendship and our companionship as well as the partnership that I have been fortunate to witness between the two of you as accomplished professionals and as husband and wife.

Thank you Jay & Mary Carneal. Jay, I appreciate you for being a wise friend, a patient ear, and for offering some of the most important and utterly brilliant ideas on this project.

Thank you: Helena Meirinho, Stacy Myers, Carrie Lawson, Kim Matera, Sam Hadley, Sheri McClain, Jerry & Nina Palmer, Craig & Debbie Guido, Robin & Wynn Jordan, Ray Smith, Arlene Gooch, Anais Malone, Bonnie Childress, Carla Savage, Tracie Spencer, Vanessa Copeland, Karen Hicks, Darren Tutt, TT Torrez, Clovia Lawrence, Shane Roberts-Thomas, Beverly Dedeaux, Carolyn Martin, Renee Robinson, Wyndi Robertson, Brian Robertson, Nathan Thomas, Carrie Dean, Alicia Miller, Marsha Landess, Linda Forem, Rosetta Devine, Mikki Spencer, Tanya Allsbrooks, Shavonne Smith, Adrian Edmondson, Bob Walden, Chris Walker, Michele Green, Kevin Bledsoe, Jim Minor, Janel St. John, J.R. Davis, Bo Jackson, Gayle Hobson, Juanita Barnes-Lewis, Sean Anthony, Keith Jones, Bilal Morris, Rodney Stevens, Mitch Malone, Jeff Anderson, Cameron Cooper, Steve Lilly, Chris Lawless, Kim Morris, Adam & Brenda Drudge, Reggie & Shaba Baker, Antionette Essa, Tracy Foard, Lisa Marion, Sue Kennedy, Lisa Reed, Wendy Gerst, Sheila Belle, Brittany Johnson, Lawrence Dunford, Mark & Kim Perkins, and Tanisha Bagley for being steadfast in your acquaintanceships, in your friendships, and in your support of this project. Your continued fellowship is as priceless to me as your courage, your honesty, and your selflessness.

友谊

Introduction

"All relationships, platonic or intimate, share a common road of evolution. Most of us have repeatedly lost our way for want of good directions . Here is the compass that will help you avoid some of the unintended detours, the u-turns, the snarls, and the dead ends that keep us from reaching our desired destination."

Robert E. Hall

Newsflash! Relationships - particularly the romantic type - do NOT have to be 'dead-ends' or 'all-or-nothing' propositions that leave you feeling: trapped, unappreciated, unfulfilled, misunderstood, deceived, bitter, or alone?

If you are reading this book, it is likely because *you* desire and deserve to have healthy and happy relationships with others.

Question 1. How many times have *you* been attracted to someone and then pursued a friendship or a more serious relationship only to discover that *you* really didn't like them?

Question 2. Do *you* find it difficult or uncomfortable: making *new* friends? retiring (letting go of) *bad* relationships? trusting family or co-workers?

Question 3. Would *you* like to experience: more balance, more depth, more trust, more control, and more personal satisfaction in *your* social life?

I have spent the better part of the last twenty-five years stumbling through platonic and romantic relationships hoping to be a an ear of empathy, desiring to be a strong arm of support, and a assuming that I was a warm heart of tolerance and acceptance; I also expected to find others who would - in their way - understand, validate, and help *me* feel safe. In all of my emotion and ambition-driven stumbling, I had lost sight of – or, maybe I had never actually recognized - the most important feature of any successful relationship. **Friendship!**

"Don't let your desire for a relationship get ahead of your friendship."

Robert E. Hall

Like most of you, I had rushed head or heart first into early relationships of all types fueled primarily by: common interests, admiration, adoration, validation, physical attraction, social rapport, and a desire for companionship. Excitement and blind confidence *(more like naïveté)* fast forwarded me right through the early friend building phase - I assumed it was a given – straight into the companionship or partnership phases where I eventually discovered that I had not cultivated enough of a friendship to sustain the so-called relationship. Foolishly, I believed that I had learned a valuable lesson (or two) when failure ultimately came and - of course - expected to do things differently the next time. **NOT!**

"With every good-bye, we must also be willing and able to let go."

Robert E. Hall

It goes without saying that there are no error-proof relationship strategies; but, I believe that 99.9% of us would agree that it is best to begin as FRIENDS FIRST!

FRIENDS FIRST is a simple and intuitive approach to better interpersonal relationships and was written in a: **who?, how?,** and **why?** format to help minimize or to avoid the pain, the frustration, the disappointment, and the stress that we feel when relationships – particularly, the long-term ones - break down. With marriages and serious commitments failing at a rate of fifty percent or higher, it is painfully clear that the early lessons of childhood and adolescence regarding respectful communication, purposeful conflict resolution, and meaningful forgiveness have been lost, or - sadly for some - were never learned. Successful relationships require the right social skills and tools to manage the inevitabilities of difference, change, and time. FRIENDSFIRST offers the skills and the tools that will enable *you* to get to know *you* so that **YOU** are then able to get to know **ME**.

"One of the surest evidences of friendship that one individual can display to another is telling him gently of a fault. If any other can excel, it is listening to such a disclosure with gratitude, and amending the error."

Edward G. Bulwer-Lytton

FRIENDSFIRST will help *you* take ownership, assume control and accept responsibility for *your* role in every type of relationship. *You* will discover more personal happiness and learn to weave a more rewarding, balanced and vibrant social web of acquaintances, friends, and family by breaking *your* relationships down into their three primary conditions: *Friendship*, *Companionship,* and *Partnership*. Within these three conditions, *you* will also identify and better understand the three levels of *engagement*: Platonic, Intimate, and Romantic; the three levels of *affection*: Like, Love, and Lust; as well as the critical difference between *Wants* and *Needs*.

What is meant by an 'intuitive' approach?

Intuition - a term used loosely to mean many things - is most often employed as a synonym for the subconscious or instinctive processing of information. Commonly considered your sixth sense, it uses - but does not need to rely on - the information gained through your other five senses. Intuition is a natural gift each of us learns to trust in order to survive. It is what most might refer to as our *common* sense and has been essential to the management of every relationship since grade school.

What makes FRIENDS FIRST different?

At the core, and most important to this approach, is *your* **P**ersonal **O**perating **S**ystem: the unique list of values, beliefs, experiences, fears, desires, needs, conditioning, and expectations that govern *your* behaviors. These factors – different in their combination and level of importance for each of us – define *your* character, shape *your* persona, drive *your* ambitions, and manage *your* ability to establish and build on rapport. *Your* **P. O. S.**, subsequently, determines: who *you* think *you* are; what *you* would like *others* to think of *you*; the social, physical and spiritual lines *you* might occasionally straddle; and, those lines that *you* will never cross. Further, it frames how *you* perceive, measure, and, subsequently, engage *your* immediate social environment.

"We can't solve problems by using the same kind of thinking we used when we created them."

.–Albert Einstein

The first objective in FRIENDS FIRST is to identify the 'authentic' *you*. "Who are *you*? What do *you* want? What do *you* need? What do *you* fear?"

Second. FRIENDS FIRST establishes simple and clear definitions of: <u>Friendship</u> - *the foundation of all healthy social bonding*, <u>Companionship,</u> and <u>Partnership</u>. A better understanding of the respective conditions of 'relationship' helps *you* to manage *your* actions and *your* expectations, and, allows *you* to effectively adjust from one condition to another, and back, if necessary.

"Will love last longer if *you* are FRIENDS FIRST?"

"Definitely," says New York social psychologist Dr. Grace Cornish-Livingstone. "*As friends first, you <u>like</u> each other first. You develop* a _respect_ for each other. You're looking out for each other's _best interests_. I urge people--marry your best friend."

Dr. Cornish-Livingstone, author of best-selling relationship books like: _'You deserve healthy love, Sis!'_ says that love, kindness, and respect equal friendship.

"You're always kind to your friend. You're looking out for his or her best interest. In a friendship you're equally grounded. You're not looking for any kind of ownership. There's no respect if you become possessive and controlling."

"Friendship is especially important for love to last longer when it comes to marriage", says Dr. Cornish-Livingstone. _"Marriage takes place long before the wedding. The wedding is the celebration, but the marriage and initial bonding should have started long before. If you have a genuine friendship, you're not going to pretend to be someone you're not so that a person can marry you. Some people are on their best behavior until they cross the threshold. Then, they let their guards down. But your true nature will surface when you're a person's friend first. When you're true friends from the beginning, you don't have to pretend."_

What is 'friending'?

While used most commonly to describe online social activity, it is employed here to describe all deliberate verbal and non-verbal efforts of communicating with acquaintances and friends. _Friending_ is as subtle as practiced cordiality and as overt as direct flirtation and good-natured teasing. It is: play-dates, birthday parties, nights out with the girls, poker with the guys, book clubs, karaoke, confiding, and even consoling. _Friending_ - done properly - employs personal honesty and should always encourage unfiltered dialogue, trust, and the feeling of unconditional acceptance.

When sincere and consistent, a basic level of trust - the core of all healthy and valued relationships - is born and that offer of trust is encouraged through continued veracious dialogue. The key is to avoid the self-serving and protectionist habits that most of us practice early on. During the early _friending_ phase, the _authentic_ you must feel empowered to say who _you_ REALLY are and what *you* REALLY want. *Your* friendship becomes more valuable when others are able to see that *you* 'walk your talk' and that *you* encourage the same for *them*.

Learning to be a <u>valued</u> friend is the foundation of FRIENDS FIRST. True friendships are the most important relationships we have. They are entered into on a voluntary basis and are maintained by mutual and respectful consent. If we believe that the best relationships are between the best of friends, learning to be a <u>better</u> friend is a deliberate and ultimately rewarding act.

What are the 'gray' areas?

Respecting and managing the often complicated *gray* areas that exist between the different relationship conditions is essential to *your* overall relationship health. Not everyone that goes from *acquaintance* to becoming a *friend* desires to be a *companion*; similarly, not every *companion* desires to evolve the relationship into a *partnership* with specific commitments and expectations. Accepting the *gray* areas that exist for some without attempting to change their heart or mind is the highest form of respect. Anything else can be interpreted as self-serving and manipulative. FRIENDS FIRST is not meant to be a tool to fix or adjust the behavior of *others*; instead, it forces *you* to take ownership of *your* role within any relationship condition.

What is 'personal branding'?

Branding and its associated terms or phrases are meant to help you further identify *your* social style (the unique and sometimes complex mix of intellect, passions, expressions, interests, talents, values, and needs) as well as the style of current or potential relationship partners.

Interestingly, Hollywood uses **friending, gray areas** and **branding** to great effect in <u>film:</u> 'Sex and the city', 'It's complicated', 'He's just not that into you', 'Brothers', 'Alfie', 'Hitch', 'Brown sugar, 'The Best Man', 'Love Jones', 'The Good girl', 'Thelma and Louise', 'Woman on top', 'High Fidelity', 'My best friend's wedding', 'There's something about Mary', 'The breakup',

'Boomerang', 'Sideways', 'Beaches, 'Boys on the side', 'Brokedown palace', 'Steel magnolias', and 'When Harry met Sally'; and in <u>TV:</u> 'Three's company', 'The odd couple', 'Seinfeld', 'Two and a half men', 'accidentally on purpose', 'Grey's anatomy', "the big bang theory', 'how I met your mother', 'Ugly Betty', 'Modern family', 'Desperate housewives', and 'Friends'.

At the end of each step, we will look at how our friends *'**You***'* *(male bear)* and *'**Me***'* *(female bear)* are dealing with the relationship concerns covered in this book that affect: their workplace, their family and their friendship with each other.

'You' and *'Me'*

Finally! If you are feeling out of balance, unappreciated, defensive and a little gun-shy as a result of the hit-or-miss of relationship building, this book is for you!

FRIENDS FIRST offers the healthiest and most rewarding method of managing *your* part in the good, the bad and the ugly of *your* relationships by reminding *you* to be prepared to reconcile, to reward, and - occasionally - to retire relationships regardless of whether they are platonic, romantic, or intimate.

"Want better relationships? Become a better friend!"

友谊

The 'epiphany'

"At the end of my days, I hope to look back and celebrate a legacy of genuine friends, of faithful companions, and of trusted partners in good times and bad. They were - and remain - my real and incalculable wealth.

Collectively, my friends have made my life meaningful and they have revealed to me the beauty of the human soul.

I know now that it is not the pursuit of a single relationship that has made my life worth living, but rather, the sum of them all."

Robert E. Hall

友谊

"Some of the biggest challenges in relationships come from the fact that most people enter a relationship in order to get something. They're trying to find someone who's going to make them feel good. In reality, the only way a relationship will last is if you see your relationship as a place that you go to give, and not a place that you go to take."

Anthony Robbins

Part I   Relationships

The first step: relationship 'conditions'...what are they?

FRIENDS FIRST begins the process of understanding, and, subsequently, improving the quality of *your* relationships by breaking them down into three specific: relationship **conditions,** types of physical **involvement,** and levels of emotional **affection.**

1.1   The 'friendship' condition

Question: What are *we* saying when *we* call someone a friend?

The first and most important relationship condition is friendship. It establishes and maintains the foundation of all of our other healthy and productive involvements and requires the exchanging of interests, experiences, trust, and concern. Friendships don't just happen; they are neither a matter of convenience nor of popularity. Real friendships take time and typically have three stages of growth.

Our acquaintanceships, or those 'pre-friendships' in the initial **stimulus** stage, can blossom when we experience physical and verbal rapport, a sense of mutual respect, and some shared interests.

In the second or **value** stage, *we* have come to appreciate and respect intangible things like: ethics, character, and morals.

2

The third, and most intimate expression of an evolving friendship, is the **role** stage where *we* share: family, specific activities, dreams, fears, support, and some measure of responsibility to and for each other.

Take a proactive attitude when initiating or building upon friendships. Do not hesitate to use affirmative language to assure new friends or to reassure established friends of *their* importance. Be mindful that not all friendships are equal and should differences or conflicts arise in the two relationship conditions that follow, you should do your best to work through those challenges from your foundation as friends.

1.2   The 'companionship' condition

Definition: *associating with or accompanying another*

The second - and maybe the most cherished - relationship condition is *companionship*. As trust grows, friends and acquaintances begin to explore their 'natural' rapport (section 3.2) beyond limited verbal interactions and, subsequently, make formal plans to share events, activities, and other friends. Usually, one acquaintance or friend will extend an invitation to the other to attend or to be a part of something the inviter enjoys and has reason to believe the invitee will as well.

Barring social conflict or a break in trust, 'natural' rapport and common interests typically offer repeated opportunities to share meaningful experiences.

The joy of the companionship condition is in the sharing of space, events, other friends, occasions, and in the feeling of camaraderie for short *(companionship of opportunity)* or long *(companionship of understanding)* periods of time. Best of all, companionship does <u>not</u> require a romantic or intimate involvement.

1.3   The 'partnership' condition

<u>Definition</u>: *one associated with another, especially in an agreed upon action*

The third and most involved relationship condition is *partnership*. It requires the highest level of trust as it is based on expectations, understandings, or agreements between two people. It matters little whether the partners are roommates, doubles partners in tennis, business associates, band members, domestic partners, or spouses. Entering a partnership of any kind should be done with mature fore-thought, honesty, and open communication. It should be devoid of any form of ultimatum or coercion. If the foundation of your friendship has been shaky before a partnership has been mutually agreed upon, make the concerted effort to build that base of trust before making commitments or promises that may potentially be broken.

Partnerships - bilateral by design - come with conditions and expectations that friendships and companionships do not. Your partner may expect one or more of the following types of support: physical, financial, spiritual, or emotional. This is where honest communication in the early stages of the *friending* process can minimize the chances of feeling: misunderstood, neglected, trapped or unimportant. **Remember this.** The perfect partner is <u>NOT</u> a perfect person! Do not make, imply, solicit, coerce, or infer promises that *you* do not desire or that *you* cannot keep. Which statement best describes *your* partnership?

"I feel that I am or that I can become who I am truly meant to be; I feel trusted and respected, and I do not fear rejection or abandonment."

4

"In order to be with you, I feel that I must compromise who I am or who I may become; I am not sure of just what I may expect and I do not feel safe or valued."

1.4   The three types of 'involvement':

<blockquote>Definition: to take part in; to interact with intent</blockquote>

The definitions that follow are composites and may differ slightly depending on cultural influences and/or religious beliefs. The objective in identifying the levels of engagement is to establish a better understanding as to just how they differ from each other so that *you* may be better able to make clear and timely decisions regarding *your* desired level of involvement.

Platonic

<blockquote>Definition: a non-sexual affectionate relationship not subject to gender pairings and including close relatives.</blockquote>

Romantic

<blockquote>Definition: refers to a very close relationship between friends who are physically and/or spiritually attracted to each other; words of deep affection and passion are spoken frequently, and interaction often involves a degree of physical closeness such as holding hands and cuddling, but not necessarily including sexual contact.</blockquote>

Intimate

Platonic relationships are simple enough to manage and seldom become complicated; they grow and are carried along by a respectful, continuous, and mutual choice to share the uncomplicated joy of another's company.

Before engaging in **romantic** or **intimate** behaviors, take the time to be certain that *you* and *your* friend are of like-mind. While intimacy and romance sound very similar in their connotations, - and are often intertwined - the expectations for each and the levels of trust desired or needed may be very different from person to person.

Many lengthy relationships have seemingly survived on romance alone; and, the same can be said – although much less often – of those sharing intimacy. The likelihood is that those relationships that endure continue to observe and to appreciate the simple joys and the respect found primarily in platonic relationships.

Misunderstandings - created by differing wants or needs or by differing interpretations - happen often and easily and can damage the trust that is the foundation of *your* relationship. Those wants or needs should be expressed early, often, and clearly to ensure that mutual relationship desires have been identified and agreed upon.

1.5   The three levels of 'affection':

Definition: *fondness or tender feelings towards another*

Like, **Love**, and **Lust** are clearly very different levels of affection and should be foremost in *your* thought process when building relationships. Do not assume that *your* desires are either understood or mutual; and, at no time and under no circumstance should expectations be created without first verbally identifying *your* desired level of affection.

Like

Definition: *to find agreeable or enjoyable*

Love

Definition: *a deep affection or fondness; to greatly cherish*

Lust

Definition: *strong sexual desire*

Let's say that an involvement begins as a mutually lusty tryst *(known as visceral sex)* and is driven primarily by physical attraction. The intimate participants would be wise to acknowledge <u>that</u> fact early on *before* ever-changing romantic sensibilities have a chance to <u>rewrite</u> the story and misrepresent the true genesis of the relationship.

In time, a very respectful, committed and emotion-based partnership *(known as relational sex)* may certainly evolve. What is the caveat of a lust-born or visceral relationship? Make sure that it is not being <u>offered</u> or <u>accepted</u> as a substitute for <u>real intimacy</u>; and, remember that deepening feelings for one may NOT be shared or returned in the same way. What is important is to appreciate the differences between the stages of affection and to understand that LIKE and - ultimately - LOVE, together, offer the greatest chance at <u>long-term</u> happiness.

Elaine and G. William Walster - in their book *'A new look at love'* - remind *us* that the affection of love can appear in two very different forms: **passionate** love and **companionate** love.

<u>Passionate</u> love can be a wildly emotional state; a confusion of feelings: tenderness and sexuality, elation and pain, anxiety and relief, altruism and jealousy.

<u>Companionate</u> love, on the other hand, is lower-keyed. It is an abiding and friendly affection as well as a deep attachment to someone. This is the type of love that forms the basis of long-lasting relationships

1.6   **Wants** and **needs**. *"are they different?"*

Dr. Willard F. Harley, in his book *'His needs, Her needs'* identifies below some of the 'similar but different' primary <u>wants</u> and <u>needs</u> of both men and women.

<u>Her</u> primary wants and needs:

Affection

Conversation

Honesty and openness

Financial support

Family commitment

<u>His</u> primary wants and needs:

Sexual fulfillment

Recreational companionship

Attractive companion

Domestic support

Admiration/respect

While it is not expected of *you* in acquaintanceships and platonic friendships, it is, nonetheless, worthwhile to take the initiative early on and share *your* wants and *your* needs with <u>romantic</u> and <u>intimate</u> partners.

Friendship, above all else, is supposed to be a relationship of equals, with trustworthiness and camaraderie flowing more readily between those *we* feel are peers. Open, honest, and respectful communication about <u>identifiable</u> wants or needs improves the capacity for trust, acceptance, and intimacy.

Let us begin with how **'You'** *(the male bear)* and **'Me'***(the female bear)* first met.

You and **Me**
on *relationship conditions*

A co-worker and mutual acquaintance named **'Him'** invited them both to his annual New Years Eve party. Before that evening, **You** and **Me** had only exchanged polite smiles and very brief but cordial greetings as they passed each other in the hallways of their very large mutual employer *'BEARZ R US'*. Neither knew the other's name and - despite their mutual attraction - felt comfortable enough to initiate an introduction.

Upon unexpectedly encountering **You** at the party, **Me** experienced a feeling - as she would later reveal - likened to 'the sun rising on the most beautiful Spring day'. There was an immediate non-verbal sense of <u>rapport</u>. Feeling considerably more comfortable outside of the office, **You** decided to break the conversational ice with the attractive and visibly nervous **Me**.

"It's so nice to finally meet the lady behind that beautiful smile!" shouted **You** over the loud music. **Me** blushed and extended her hand. *"I can be a little shy at first, but I warm up pretty quickly. It's nice to finally meet you too!"*

For the first time in a very long while, **You** was at a loss for words. He was captivated but tried hard not to stare. Like magnets, they were being drawn physically closer and their curious eyes continually met with an unmistakable warmth and approval.

The two chatted on through the evening and discovered that **Him** - the co-worker hosting the party - had been a mutual acquaintance of both for about the same length of time. **You** shared that **Him** was on his bowling and volleyball league teams and that they occasionally went fishing together.

*"So, you're good friends with **Him**"*, inquired **Me**? **You** scratched his head as he smiled and pondered the question. *"Hmmmm,...It probably looks that way, but actually, we are still just acquaintances who enjoy some of the same things. I guess you could call it a <u>companionship of opportunity</u>."*

Me nodded with understanding. Looking in the direction of the host**,** she begins to share that she has had a crush on **Him** since they were college classmates and that they actually went out on a few dates. *"I don't think that I can actually call **Him** and I friends either. We usually get along just great but there isn't a real basis for a friendship yet. I guess you might say that we're <u>companions of understanding</u>"* she says with a chuckle. **You** nods and smiles broadly.

Looking down at her feet, **Me** wistfully acknowledges that she had hoped for more but that she never got the impression that **Him** wanted a relationship of any real significance and, as it has turned out, that was just fine with her.

"I am glad that I came tonight" exclaims a smiling **You** over the loud music. *"I hope that this is the beginning of a beautiful <u>acquaintanceship</u>!?"* Her face in full blush and warmed by his quick wit, **Me** adjusts her glasses and leans in to whisper; *"so do I!"*

友谊

"It's surprising how many persons go through life without ever recognizing that their feelings toward other people are largely determined by their feelings toward themselves; and, if you're not comfortable within yourself, you can't be comfortable with others."

Sidney J. Harris

Part II   Discover *You*, Discover *Me*

The second step: Who are *'you'*? *really?*

For most of *us*, it can take a lifetime to answer that question honestly and completely. It is very important to acknowledge that *we* each desire - on many levels - to experience healthy relationships with others. Healthy relationships require that *we* know ourselves at *our* core and that *we* be able to share that knowledge.

Susan Piver, in her book *'The hard questions: the 100 essential questions to ask before you say I do',* shares a very real, common, and often troubling crossroad that she - like many of *us* - reached in her own relationship.

When her best friend and partner Duncan asked her to marry, she immediately tried to break up with him! She loved this man and adored her five year relationship; but, she knew all too well from previous experiences that feelings - including her own - change. How could she promise to love and be contented and committed to Duncan - or anyone for that matter - for the rest of her life?

With great trepidation, she suggested a one month separation to think things over. After intense reflection and honest internal dialogue regarding the pros and cons of marriage and her own *individual* wants and needs (section 1.6), Susan realized that *she* saw marriage as a partial retirement of her vibrant and adventurous life. Instead of being able to roam every square foot of a beautiful dream home, she saw herself being confined to one room with only one view. Duncan's proposal had brought her face to face with the best of her individual truths and the worst of her relationship fears. That one room and that one view would never be enough!

After a month, Susan and Duncan decided to get together for a weekend. She was now ready to share her truths (section 3.1) and her fears (section 1.6) without expectation and - more importantly - was prepared for any outcome. Susan was not ready to be a traditional wife. Duncan listened with great patience and openness until she was finished. He handed her a small heart-shaped box. Inside it were a rock and a feather.

"The rock is me; you are the feather. Fly! Let me be constant and steady. Let's hold it all in one heart. Let us balance each other!"

It was a beautiful and complex message of unconditional love and acceptance. Susan was in awe. The man that she loved had found a way - in those simple words - to: express his capacity to love, to grow her love for him and to show her another level she did not think possible in committed relationships. For the first time, she was able to believe that marriage could enhance her life as well as strengthen her. Susan no longer feared 'one room with a view'. Most importantly, she had finally been able to express *her* greatest relationship fears and find acceptance and understanding.

Susan said yes to Duncan's proposal by promising him what she desired to do and what she knew she could do. She promised to act 'lovingly' towards him for the rest of her life. She explained that to 'act lovingly' means being painfully honest and accountable to ourselves and to our partners without exception.

Dr. Phillip C. McGraw, opens his book *'Relationship Rescue',* with the no-nonsense first step of 'getting real'. He emphasizes that nothing good or lasting can happen until you do. Until *you* have successfully discovered or taken back *your* power and become the kind of person who commands respect instead of demanding it, *you* will find it difficult to truly connect with anyone; and, it will be even more difficult to reconnect when conflicts arise.

Online relationship sites like **eHarmony** and **match.com**, with over twenty million subscribers, use tools like their respective *compatibility matching systems* to screen across as many as 29 dimensions of compatibility. Their systems try to cut through affectation and apathy and are thorough and insightful in the types of questions asked; thus, honesty and candor are expected of a subscriber in order for the tools to be effective.

The online relationship sites ask specific questions and offer their users a chance to answer those questions honestly and without the fear of immediate rejection or judgment; a first for most of their subscribers. I highly recommend that *you* complete one of these, or a similar type of relationship profile in an effort to gain greater clarity on just how hard it is to be completely honest with yourself; be willing to express just how specific *your* wants and needs (section 1.6) truly are.

2.1 What is *your* 'Personal Operating System'?

> Definition: programming that: directs the input and output of data, keeps track of historical information, controls and manages physical systems, serves as the interface between the physical systems and the user, allocates resources to various functions, and acts as a host for new information and advanced programming.

This structured sounding definition of an operating system is not so very different from what *your* conscious and subconscious minds *(software/user)* do for *your* bodies *(hardware/physical systems)*.

Like a computer, *your* **P. O. S.** *(conscious and subconscious minds)* is capable of running and managing many programs simultaneously. Some of them run continuously and are located on the *survival/security/needs* hard drive *(subconscious mind)* while others run when needed and are located in *your values/lessons/growth* programs *(conscious mind)*.

Your **P. O. S.** is both a rule book and the blueprint of *your* social style (section 2.4) and is governed by a complex combination of socio-economic factors and emotional conditioning (section 6.4); the latter is both inherited and learned, and will continue to evolve over time. Below is a sample list of those factors and conditioning.

Faith/Belief system	Culture/traditions
Family history/values	Fears/handicaps
Confidence/Self esteem	Desires/needs/ambitions
Success/accomplishments	Status/education

Life experiences/age	Pleasure/pain
Interests/hobbies/talents	Empathy/indifference
Security/survival	Integrity/character

Using this list of factors, *your* **P. O. S.** filters and processes new information daily in order to: govern *your* thoughts, frame *your* opinions and feelings, and, subsequently, determine the suitable course of action or reaction.

Just as a computer uses its operating system to produce output from the interaction of its various programs, humans are continuously doing the same. We differ in a very important way however in that we are *self* aware. *Our* **P. O. S.** can produce complex results that - at times - simultaneously compliment and conflict us. Because we are *self* aware, we are able to represent those compliments and conflicts in visual and auditory packages that *we* can identify as personal **brands** (section 2.2).

2.2   What is *your* 'brand'? *"yes, you have at least one!"*

Personal branding is typically represented in both affirmative and active terms; it expresses - through visual, auditory, and kinesthetic forms - what *you* think is best about the data that *your* **P. O. S.** continuously processes. Branding is used to describe the unique mix of *your* tangible and intangible *goods* (social style - section 2.4) and how *you* physically manifest those goods through *your* communication portals (section 3.2).

In describing *you*, friends or acquaintances may use partial branding terms or phrases such as: 'life of the party', 'jack of all trades', 'go-getter', 'super woman', 'old soul', or 'Renaissance man' to capture some observable elements of *your* **P. O. S.** Branding can run the gamut of the serious to the silly and the brash to the benign, but - ultimately - it helps to present a clearer and deeper understanding of just who *you* are. It explains why *you* can have friends who connect with *you* but who are very different from each other.

Listed on the following page are some examples of personal brands. The brevity of their descriptions belies the fact that brands are indeed complex mixes of: likes and dislikes, strengths and weaknesses, talents and skills, experiences and interests, as well as personality and social style. Be mindful to establish personal honesty at the core of *your* brand mix (section 2.0). In so doing, *you* help prevent y*our* brand(s) from becoming faddish or complete imitations of those *you* socialize with, admire or favor. *Your* brands should represent a clear understanding of the message(s) that *you* feel comfortable broadcasting publicly.

Try these **alliterative** descriptions of <u>brands</u> on for size:

18

Liberal and lively

Conservative and charming

Smart and stylish

Confident and classy

Unpredictable and urbane

Honest and humble

Worldly and wise

Artistic and active

Loyal and loving

Driven and dramatic

Idealistic and intense

Cheerful and comforting

Bright and beautiful

Sassy and sagacious

Talented and timeless

Soulful and sapient

Outspoken and original

Bold and brilliant

Funny and flirty

Intelligent and introspective

Elegant and engaging

Below is a list of both the noteworthy and the famous. They have successfully used *their* brand(s) to clarify *their* personal lives and to enhance *their* public and professional images:

Donald Trump, Oprah Winfrey, Charles Barkley, Paris Hilton, Kim Kardashian, Simon Cowell, Paula Abdul, Ann Coulter, Muhammad Ali, George Foreman, Steven Tyler, Paula Deen, Queen Latifah, Judge 'Judy' Sheindlin, Magic Johnson, John McEnroe, Sean 'diddy' Combs, Martha Stewart, Howard Stern, Ben Stein, Hulk Hogan, Jesse James, Dr. Phil, Rachel Ray, Hugh Hefner, George Steinbrenner, Jerry Jones, John Madden, Bill Cosby, Madonna, Whoopi Goldberg, Omarosa, Lady Gaga, Kim Kardashian, Dwayne 'The Rock' Johnson, Shaquille O'neil, Dr. Oz, Tiger Woods, Michael Jordan, Walter Cronkite, Bob Villa, Gen. Colin Powell, Sarah Palin, Arianna Huffington, Rush Limbaugh, Larry King, Earl Nightingale, Napoleon Hill, Dale Carnegie, Charles Schwab, Jimmy Buffet, Albert Einstein, and Arnold Schwarzenegger.

2.2.1 Can *you* have <u>more</u> than one brand?

The answer is an unequivocal **YES!** Most of *us* have <u>multiple</u> brands depending on a mix of any number of factors such as: *our* lifestyle, *our* level of maturity, *our* employment, *our* current social circumstance, *our* immediate mood, or a particular occasion. It is important to understand that gaining clarity on *your* brand(s) is the key to identifying (visually), describing (verbally), and expressing (physically) *you* in simpler terms known as <u>word</u> pictures. *Your* brand *'mix'* always manifests itself physically and is <u>revealed</u> in combinations of the following twelve expressions:

Your walk	Your talk	Your writing	Your clothing
Your grooming	Your body art	Your social affiliations	Your music and books
Your hobbies and interests	Your personal vehicles	Your sports and pets	Your home décor

Try selecting at least three 'brand' descriptors (from the list on page 19) that *you* think most closely represent how *you* - and others - tend to see *you*. You can mix and match the various adjectives to create the most <u>accurate</u> word pictures. If *you* are able to <u>verbally</u> express to a friend *your* choice of descriptors and how they best represent who *you* are, *you* have successfully understood that *we* all have more than one dimension. It is healthy and purposeful for each of *us* to continually evolve and - sometimes - to even reinvent ourselves. *Our* friendships and relationships can grow more meaningfully when *we* are able to find acceptance. Unfortunately, socio-economic influences, the fears, the restrictions, and the judgments of others can hinder *our* journey to self discovery. The objective in identifying, verbalizing, and living *your* brand(s) is to enhance and to experience healthy rapport with others (section 3.2). ***"People like people who are most like them".*** *Your* brand(s) make it easier for like-minded people to recognize and to try and establish rapport with *you*.

2.3　What is *your* 'social style'?

Each of *us* exhibits a <u>pattern of behavior</u> that can be identified and responded to. Understanding this, *you* can - with a little effort - increase *your* chances of successful communication and interaction in any relationship condition. The name given to *your* observable <u>pattern(s) of behavior</u> - the 'public' *you* - is your **social style**.

Your **social style** is strongly influenced by two very important dimensions of human behavior: **assertiveness** *(telling, asking)* and **responsiveness** *(reacting, controlling, expressing, displaying).* How these two dimensions are <u>paired</u> *(more assertive/less expressive, less assertive/less expressive, more assertive/more expressive, less expressive/more assertive)* determine which <u>social style</u> *you* tend to exhibit.

Understanding that *you* tend to - but not absolutely - fall into a particular **social style**, it is then important to accept that *you* should control *your* behaviors instead of trying to control or modify the behavior of *others*. Make it a habit to be proactive instead of reactive. Reactive behavior can lead to defensiveness and can allow a simple phrase or a missed gesture to negate the best of rapport or spontaneity. Proactive behavior helps *you* to remain in control of what *you* say and of what *you* do.

Recognizing *your* dominant **social style** helps *you* to take more responsibility in *your* relationships and helps *you* to avoid misunderstanding, discomfort, and conflict. The four styles listed below - as identified by David W. Merrill and Roger H. Reid in *'Personal styles & effective performance'*, and by Gary Smalley in *'Hidden Keys to loving relationships'* - will help *you* to determine *your* style and that of *your* relationship partners.

It should be noted that one style is not <u>better</u> than another. Success in relationships depends greatly on *your* ability to be cognizant of *your* own style and to be versatile (section 2.8) enough to establish rapport with someone of a differing style. ***"Which are you?"***

Amiable / *Golden retriever* *(Less assertive/more responsive)*

<u>Strengths:</u> supportive, respectful, willing, dependable, agreeable, loyal

<u>Weaknesses:</u> conforming, unsure, pliable, dependent, awkward

<u>Famous Amiables:</u> Oprah; Pres. Jimmy Carter; Mother Theresa; Ellen Degeneres; Laura Bush; Maya Angelou; Barbara Walters; Patti Labelle; Captain Kanagroo; Ghandi; Bill Cosby; Princess Diana

Amiables tend to 'ask' and 'show' emotions.

Expressive / *Otter* *(More responsive/more assertive)*

<u>Strengths:</u> ambitious, stimulating, enthusiastic, friendly

<u>Weaknesses:</u> manipulative, undisciplined, reacting, egotistical

<u>Famous Expressives:</u> Eddie Murphy; Joan Rivers; Terry Bradshaw; Regis Philbin; Tony Curtis; Magic Johnson; Bob Hope; Robin Williams; Lucille Ball; Pres. Bill Clinton; Carol Burnette; Jim Carrey

Expressives tend to 'tell' and 'show' emotions.

Driver / *Lion* *(More assertive/less responsive)*

Strengths: strong willed, independent, practical, decisive, efficient

Weaknesses: pushy, severe, tough, dominating, harsh

Famous Drivers: Donald Trump; Clint Eastwood; Hillary Clinton; Martha Stewart; Condoleezza Rice; Vince Lombardi; Napoleon; Pres. Richard Nixon; Henry Ford

Drivers tend to 'tell' and 'control' emotions.

Analytical / *Beaver* *(less assertive/less responsive)*

Strengths: industrious, persistent, serious, exacting, orderly

Weaknesses: critical, indecisive, stuffy, picky, moralistic

Famous Analyticals: Dr. Phillip C. McGraw; Judge Judith Sheindlin; General Colin Powell; Alan Greenspan; Albert Einstein; Pres. Woodrow Wilson; Agatha Christie

Analyticals tend to 'ask' and 'control' emotions.

2.4   Recognizing the <u>four</u> social styles.

Amiables or *Golden Retrievers*: Relationship oriented

Amiables tend to place a high priority on friendships, close relationships, approval, and cooperative behavior. They often lend joy, warmth, and spontaneity to social situations. They tend to enjoy traditions and sentimentality. They are keen in spotting what they believe to be personal motives in relationships. Amiables will use understanding and mutual respect to achieve cooperative goals whenever possible versus power. A focus on the present is normal as is a tendency to move at a slower pace due to their social nature. Amiables are less inclined to take risks and tend to stick with the comfortable and the known. They are trusting and expect *you* to keep *your* promises. Amiables are more comfortable asking for permission than for forgiveness. In a word, they are 'agreeable'.

Expressives or *Otters*: Intuition oriented

Expressives are typically communicative, animated, warm, approachable, and competitive. They tend to involve others in their thoughts and feelings and desire acceptance. They can sometimes conscript friends into the roles of followers and personal supporters of *their* dreams. Expressives consider power and politics important since they seek to gain *personal* recognition. Their relationships can too often seem shallow and short-lived. Expressives spend most of their time moving towards some dream of the future. They can act quickly but are usually undisciplined in their use of time. They are willing to take risks based solely on an opinion. Expressives are visionaries and tend to be highly imaginative and creative. They are more comfortable asking for forgiveness than for permission. In a word, expressives are 'stimulating'.

Drivers or *Lions*: Action oriented

Drivers tend to give the overall impression that they know what they want, where they are going, and how to get there quickly. *"Let's get it done"* is typically their motto. Drivers tend to be more focused on results than on pleasing others. They can seem uncommunicative, independent, competitive, and cool in their interactions with others. They are inclined to take the initiative and don't always see the need to explain *their* motives. Drivers tend to be focused on the tasks at hand, are risk takers, and prefer to work autonomously. They are more comfortable asking for forgiveness than for permission. In a word, drivers are 'efficient '.

Analyticals or *Beavers*: Thinking oriented

Analyticals tend to live their lives according to facts, principles, and logic. They tend to be cautious about extending friendship or showing personal warmth. They take their relationships seriously even if it is not immediately evident. A *'show me'* posture is often taken with change and leadership. Trust must be earned. Analyticals use their time in a deliberate and disciplined manner. They prefer facts to flashiness and tend to avoid unnecessary risks. Analyticals are more comfortable asking for permission than for forgiveness. In a word, they are 'accurate'.

These four styles can be used to characterize the *observable* behavior of most human beings; and, while at times people will combine the behaviors of several of the styles, an individual's basic *social style* represents his or her system for coping with relationships encountered in the course of a normal day.

2.5 What <u>message</u>(s) is *your* social style sending out?

After identifying *your* dominant *social style*, *you* can begin to understand what kinds of messages that *you* are sending out and how they might be interpreted by others. Remember this. There is no bad style; only a failure or a resistance to be flexible and versatile.

If *you* want *your* message to be well received, speak in the <u>language</u> of *your* audience. It matters little that it sounds or feels good to *you* if it does not sound or feel good to *them*.

2.6 How does social style <u>affect</u> *your* relationships?

The negative effect of conflicting or non-complimentary social styles can be both subtly and overtly cumulative. If *you* are frequently at odds with others or *you* continually feel misunderstood, rapport has little chance to grow. It would be wise for *you* to take the early initiative of 'tuning in' to verbal and non-verbal clues of *their* particular social style.

Disconnects or breakdowns are seldom one-sided. Again; this is not a discussion on changing the behavior of <u>others</u>; it is on *you* learning to be more cognizant and, subsequently, to be more <u>socially versatile</u>.

2.7 How can *you* make *your* social style more versatile?

Versatility truly is the key. Those who have learned to control *their* behavioral preferences or social styles so as to allow *their* brand(s) to establish rapport with a differing brand(s) or social style(s) are able to create, grow and maintain valuable interpersonal relationships.

The 'expressive' and the 'driver' - for example - may begin with listening and observing more and controlling less. For the 'amiable' and the 'analytical', it may help them to share in the enthusiasm or the sense of urgency of the 'driver' or the 'expressive'.

Social versatility is the undeniable key to all successful relationships. It is the *art* of rapport and the *skill* of friending in concert with one another and will be discussed further in step 3.

Below are some examples of the 4 social styles in action. Circle the style (**B GR L O**) that *you* think best fits the brief description. Refer back to the descriptions found in section 2.4 if needed.

1. Chandler is the loquacious life of the party and always seems full of new business ideas. **B GR L O**

2. Ann is our unflappable office manager and does a great job of keeping the peace.   **B GR L O**

3. Intensely ambitious, Christopher can be a little pushy, but he is efficient and knows how to get things done.
   B GR L O

4. Cayden's obsessive attention to detail is what makes this report so comprehensive.   **B GR L O**

5. With the company for over 20 years, Isaiah is reliable and even-tempered.   **B GR L O**

6. Ebulient, Jayla cannot decide between Drama club, pep team, or the glee club?   **B GR L O**

7. Jordan groused loudly that his friends lacked ambition and a capacity to lead.   **B GR L O**

8. Brittani can be a little tough on co-workers who are not as proficient as she.   **B GR L O**

9. Amanda is the self-appointed peacemaker in the family.

    B GR L O

10. Jerrica is routinely nominated to take charge of action committees and important company event planning.

    B GR L O

2.8   The four 'temperaments' (or humors)

In section 2.3, we introduced the four **social styles**. *You* learned to identify the important differences between the 'expressive', the 'driver', the 'analytical', and the 'amiable'. In this section *we* will explore those styles a little further by identifying *their* respective **temperaments**.

Humorism asserts that each person is born with a basic temperament as determined by which of the four humors tends to predominate in the individual. As *we* all produce each humor, there will be varying degrees of influence by each, but the effects of one is usually more evident. What follows is a very basic outline of the characteristics of each temperament as classically described. For more explicit information, you can read *'Character & Temperament'* by David Keirsey and Marilyn Bates.

Sanguine *(the expressive)*

■Self-composed ■Not given to worry ■Liberal
■Tends to follow rather than lead ■Cordial ■Peaceable
■Talkative ■Not averse to change ■Adjusts easily
■Prefers informality ■Aware of surroundings ■Impetuous
■Impulsive ■Lacking in perseverance ■Lacking in initiative
■Prone to carelessness and flightiness

Choleric *(the driver)*

Self-composed ■Not given to worry ■Persuasive ■Independent
■Rarely shows embarrassment ■ leads rather than follows
■Persistent ■ Decisive ■Dynamic ■Impetuous ■Impulsive ■Touchy ■
Prone to hypocrisy, deceit, pride, and anger

29

Melancholic *(the analytical)*

■Sensitive ■Intuitive ■Self-conscious ■Easily embarrassed
■Easily hurt ■Introspective ■Sentimental ■Moody
■Likes to be alone ■Empathetic ■Often artistic
■Often fussy and perfectionist ■Deep
■Prone to depression

Phlegmatic *(the amiable)*

■Peaceful ■Easy-going ■Deliberative ■Faithful ■Reliable
■Relatively unaffected by environment ■Reserved ■Distant
■Slow in movement ■Constant in mood ■Not prone to worry
■Prone to stagnation

An exaggerated way of understanding the four temperaments is to consider four people who see a very large and unknown object fall to earth. The Sanguine talks about it animatedly to all present; the Choleric wants to form an expedition to find it and analyze it; the Melancholic ponders what it means and how he or she feels about it; and, the Phlegmatic waits for the others to decide what to do as whatever decision *they* make is fine.

It's helpful and can be fun to analyze friends and acquaintances - even characters *we* see in movies - in terms of these four temperaments. Consider **'Sex and the city'** with its *Sanguine* Samantha, its *Choleric* Miranda, its *Melancholic* Carrie, and its *Phlegmatic* Charlotte.

Understanding and accepting *our* differing temperaments can help *us* better manage *our* current and *our* future relationships.

2.9 **Introverts** and **Extroverts**

"Can a relationship of opposites work?"

Two of the major <u>personality types</u> are **extroverts** and **introverts.** They tend to exist at opposite ends of the spectrum of <u>personality traits</u>. Extroverts and introverts find themselves in relationships of one kind or another with each other all the time – because opposites can attract – but may find it very difficult to build a strong relationship or marriage with each other because of communication differences.

Although relationship conflict is inevitable, resolving conflict and improving communication is easier when you understand introverted and extroverted personality types. *You* might consider taking a personality test to determine if *you're* an introvert or an extrovert but a quicker and more convenient reference is found in section 2.9.2.

Introverted Personality Traits

Introverts are territorial and usually energized by being alone, private, and quiet. Introverts are more sensitive to social rejection, feel most 'alone' when surrounded by strangers and don't always see the world as a safe place.

Emotionally <u>stable</u> introverts are:

- Passive
- Careful
- Thoughtful
- Controlled
- Reliable
- Even-tempered
- Calm

Emotionally <u>unstable</u> introverts can be:

- Quiet
- Pessimistic
- Unsociable
- Sober
- Rigid
- Moody
- Anxious
- Reserved

Extroverted Personality Traits

Extroverts tend to be energized by groups of people, conversation, and activity. Extroverts are less sensitive to rejection, and see the world as a safer place.

Emotionally <u>stable</u> extroverts are:

- Sociable
- Outgoing
- Talkative
- Responsive
- Easygoing
- Lively
- Carefree
- Leader-like

Emotionally <u>unstable</u> extroverts can be:

- Active
- Optimistic
- Impulsive
- Changeable
- Excitable
- Aggressive
- Restless
- Touchy

2.9.1   Communication 'tips' for Introverts and Extroverts in Love Relationships

Understanding *your* partner's personality traits is the key to resolving relationship conflict. The <u>introvert</u> needs to understand his/her extroverted partner's need for social activity; the <u>extrovert</u> needs to understand his/her introverted partner's need for privacy and downtime.

Finding compromise when opposites attract or when *you* have different personality traits is also important. The introvert could go to the social event with the extrovert; the extrovert could agree to leave at an earlier time. The introvert could suggest comfortable solutions to situations the extrovert enjoys, such as smaller, more intimate dinner parties instead of huge events.

Accepting *your* differences is crucial. It's one thing to understand the personality profiles of introverts and extroverts; it's another matter to actually accept or even admire different personality traits. Acceptance means the introvert doesn't try to change the extrovert and vice versa. Acceptance means the extrovert really sees the value of the introvert's personality and vice versa.

2.9.2 **Extrovert** vs **Introvert**

Extroverts are directed towards the objective world whereas Introverts are directed towards the subjective world. The most common differences between the two are shown below.

Extroverts

- are interested in what is happening around them
- are open and often talkative
- compare their own opinions with the opinions of others

Introverts

- are interested in their own thoughts and feelings
- need to have their own territory
- often appear reserved, quiet and thoughtful
- usually do not have many

33

- like action and initiative
- easily make new friends or adapt to a new group
- say what they think
- are interested in new people
- easily break unwanted relations

friends
- have difficulties in making new contacts
- like concentration and quiet
- do not like unexpected visits and therefore do not make them
- work well alone

Which are *you*?   **Extrovert ( )**   or   **Introvert ( )**

How about *your* friend/partner?

Friend	Initials	Extrovert (√)	Introvert (√)
#1			
#2			
#3			
#4			
#5			
#6			
#7			
#8			
#9			
#10			

Shortly after meeting at the New Years Eve party, our friends **You** and **Me** began to meet for an occasional lunch or movie. **Me**, still smarting from a recent breakup, and unsure of where she stood with **Him**, struggled with whether or not she should reveal her 'dating' concerns to **You**. Was it too early? Had she taken enough time to figure out what *she*

You and **Me**

on *knowing self*

truly wanted? A friend? A companion? More? Her last boyfriend thought that she was: too complex, too needy, too rigid and a bit analytical. Frustrated, he pulled away stating that he needed time to figure out what he wanted from a relationship.

You was different. He was a little older and he seemed pretty certain about who he was and what he wanted. He was confident and charming as well as worldly and wise. **You** was a natural leader and had no problem expressing his views or opinions or entertaining those of others. Best of all, he did not compromise himself nor did he patronize. **Me** found those qualities (P.O.S. Section 2.1) very appealing but worried that **You** might see *her* as un-evolved, uncommitted and fearful.

After sharing her concerns over lunch one afternoon, **Me** was encouraged by **You** to take a closer look at what *she* really wanted and needed in all of her relationships (section 1.0); at the top of the list was a desire to be more comfortable with expressing herself *(social style)* and her interests *(brands)* early and clearly.

It would seem that **You** was just who **Me** needed to start her on the all-important journey to finding her authentic self.

友谊

Stephen R. Covey

The third step: sharing the 'authentic' *you*

Definition: *not false or copied; genuine; real; that which can be believed or accepted*

3.1 Speak *your* 'truth' *'please!'*

What does that mean exactly? It is likely that most of us have either intentionally or unintentionally been sending mixed signals to those who enter *our* relationship cycle (section 5.1). That is not to say that *we* are not able to speak our minds or to speak plainly; but rather, it is to understand that *we* can easily, predictably, and often regrettably stumble when it comes to sharing our core truths. These truths are born in and arise from *your* **P. O. S.** (section 2.1)

The fear of being judged and the fear of rejection or loss are powerful inhibitors. The combinations of *our*: personal history, opinions, desires, handicaps, families, and *our* social standing can shackle the best of *us* in ways that *we* don't readily acknowledge.

Many of *us* have found *our* way through bad experiences and failed relationship conditions and on to good ones by identifying intrapersonal *(those within ourselves)* conflicts. Studies have determined that there are at least four potential problem areas associated with speaking *your* truth and with healthy relationship building:

- **Unresolved grief** – grief that is delayed and experienced long after the loss; or distorted grief in which we may not feel emotion but experience other symptoms

- **Role disputes** – occur when differing expectations about the relationship go unresolved

- **Role transitions** – occur when our roles in relationships change and we don't know how to cope with the change

- **Deficits** – result when we have problems forming and maintaining good quality relationships

The **International Society for Interpersonal Psychotherapy** offers a wealth of information on this and other matters related to managing healthy relationships.

Speaking *your* truth - as *you* have come to know it - is essential to personal honesty and to building better relationships now and in the future. If *you* are afraid of commitments, say so. If *you* desire marriage and children, say so. If *you* are still hurting or healing from a past event, say so. If *you* tend to take things very slowly and are unable to make promises, *you* must say so. Successful internet dating sites like eHarmony refer to this as *'personal disclosure'*.

Invariably, at the core of every great and lasting relationship condition is the unconditional love and acceptance of *another's* truths. *We* cannot expect to receive that gift of acceptance if *we* are not courageous enough to give it.

3.2 What is 'rapport'? *"No relationship thrives or survives for very long without it."*

> **Definition**: *when two or more parties achieve or perceive mutual harmony, trust, agreement, or commonality; a sense of mutual understanding and sympathy*

To say that a successful and fulfilling life, particularly, as it regards relationships, requires rapport is a huge understatement. It is very difficult to be: an effective leader, a loving parent, a supportive friend or a satisfying lover without the existence of rapport. Only a handful of individual goals can be achieved without it. Of the many interpersonal skills that *you* should master early in *your* social development, the *art* of rapport is both paramount and priceless.

Rapport exists when *you* experience feelings of: comfort, acceptance, trust, empathy or understanding with: an acquaintance, a friend, a co-worker, an activity partner, a spouse, or a family member. Rapport is NOT the same as physical attraction; but, physical attraction and 'personal branding' can definitely initiate and influence the desire to establish rapport.

Rapport is not born of belligerent, disrespectful, or contentious interactions; it *(natural rapport)* is discovered rather than manufactured and can be built upon with very little effort; but, for those occasions when *you* encounter someone of a differing: social style (section 2.4), language, culture, experience, generation, or ideology, *you* must be willing to make a conscious adjustment *(rapport by design)* to *your* communication dial and tune in to *their* frequency according to author and master Neuro-Linguistic Programming practitioner Nicholas Boothman. This does not, however, mean agreeing with or adopting another's beliefs or opinions. Other common hurdles to establishing rapport are: insecurity, ignorance, intolerance, peer pressure, and impatience.

Before rapport can be established, there is usually some evidence of **commonality** *(Rapport by chance)* that motivates *you* to initiate *friending* (section 4.4) behaviors. Commonality is communicated in three observable expressions: their *walk*, their *talk*, and their *chalk*. How another person comports themselves *(non-verbal, 70%)* and how they speak and write *(verbal, 30%)* affects our perception of common interests, a common language and of shared values. The highest form or experience of rapport is known as **simpatico** *(see page 148).*

"People like people who are most like themselves. That's the first rule of rapport"

Michael Brooks

Most importantly, mastering rapport is not the practice of teaching others to speak *your* language or to enjoy *your* interests, but rather a deliberate exercise in learning to speak *their* language and to show an appreciation or respect for *their* interests; by doing so, *you* offer respect, validation, and a measure of trust born of *your* displayed social versatility (section 2.8).

An effective way of developing better *(verbal)* rapport is achieved by keying in on what Neuro linguistic programming expert and author Michael Brooks calls our primary **representational** type. In his book *'Instant Rapport'*, he shares that each of us learns to interpret our surroundings and, subsequently, communicate through our five senses. One of those five senses tends to become our primary communication portal and can explain why friends are able to experience the same event differently.

On the following pages are descriptions of the three *primary* sensory (representational) communication portals.

3.3   The three communication 'portals':
"your dominant senses"

Recognizing which portals *other* people rely on to experience the world and then using this information in *your* personal, professional, and social interactions can have a tremendous effect on how quickly *you* can establish and build upon rapport.

This section identifies: the three primary sensory portals, the verbal cues used, related interests, and the social styles they are typically associated with.

The Visual

Sixty percent of us fall into this category. Visuals are inclined to be movers and shakers; they are expressive, creative and sometimes impatient. They are usually on-the-go types who are able to let go more easily of the emotional bonds that can restrain others. Visuals need to see proof or evidence before they take things seriously. Mental images come quickly and easily to them. They tend to be sharply dressed and surround themselves with attractive and interesting people and things.

We find visuals in the fields of: photography, film-making, art, architecture, design, cosmetology and landscaping. Their tendency is to speak quickly using verbal cues like: *"I see what you are saying"*, *"See you later"*, *"Can you imagine that?"*, or *"I can see myself living here."*

Their typical social style: Driver, Expressive, or Analytical

The Auditory

Auditory types relate primarily but not exclusively through sound. They are above average verbal communicators and enjoy dialogue. They can record and playback data in their minds more easily than most. They are inclined to shy away from disharmony and harsh noises. Auditory types are best approached with smooth and non-manipulative presentations. If allowed, they can easily dominate a conversation. They do not let go of relationships easily and can be very sentimental as familiar sounds such as music, laughter or a loved one's voice can hold special significance. An auditory is more inclined to 'tune in' to the communication frequency of a lover more readily than the other representational types. Auditories like to make a statement with their clothing but are not likely to stress over it.

We find these sensory types in the fields of: education, law, music, linguistics, acting, screenwriting, broadcasting, and politics. They speak at a moderate and pleasing rate and will use verbal cues like: *"I hear what you are saying"*, *"Tell me more"*, *"Does that ring a bell with you?"*, or *"That sounds good to me."*

Their typical social style: Amiable, Expressive, or Analytical

The Kinesthetic

Kinesthetics are in touch with their feelings. They tend to be very empathetic and love to *'feel'* - both internally and externally. Of the three primary types, they enjoy being in rapport most. Kinesthetics have the unique ability to convert visual and auditory dialogue into feelings. While some may mistakenly judge them to be overly sensitive, they are fiercely brave, committed and loyal. Because of their level of comfort with 'feeling', they are inclined to be good lovers and great comforters. The downside of 'feeling' so acutely is the difficultly they experience in letting go of hurt.

We find kinesthetics in the fields of: Psychology, acting, dancing, athletics, writing, plumbers, electricians, food services, and caretaking. Their rate of speech and gestures tend to be a little slower and more deliberate than the visual and the auditory and their verbal cues are: *"I have a gut feeling"*, *"I can sense that something bad is about to happen"*, *"I'm all shook up"*, *"I can't handle the pressure!"*, or *"What does your heart tell you?"*

Their typical social style: Amiable or Expressive

In his book, *'How to make people like you in 90 seconds or less'*, Nicholas Boothman offers a great analogy on becoming more aware of <u>sensory</u> types over time.

"Have you ever purchased a car...let's say a red Miata? Almost immediately, you begin to see red Miatas everywhere. Before, you had only noticed them once in a great while. Now, you start to see them where ever you go."

When you become more accomplished at distinguishing one person's dominant sensory portal from another, the same thing begins happen. That sensory type will begin to stand out to you like that red Miata.

3.4   When and why are *you* 'out' of rapport?

We often find ourselves out of rapport when we fail to identify and adapt to both the *social style* and the communication *representational type* of our audience. Learning to 'tune in' *your* attention and 'turn up' *your* interest is a good place to start. We can also find ourselves temporarily out of rapport with others on matters of deep conviction or passion such as religion, politics, sex, money, or child rearing. In these instances, when compromise or understanding is difficult to achieve, a mutual agreement to amicably and - most importantly - respectfully disagree should suffice.

Breakdowns in trust and respect can also cripple rapport. We are much less inclined to give *our* undivided attention or empathy if trust is broken or respect has been impaired. Make a concerted effort to resolve disagreements or misunderstandings quickly. More importantly, make a sincere attempt to determine as well as to understand what factor(s) from the list below caused the breakdown of rapport.

- **Emotional** - break in trust, lack of support, or feelings of abandonment

- **Physical** - break in trust, intimidation, or feelings of abandonment

- **Spiritual** - disconnect in shared beliefs, opinions, or values

- **Social** - break in trust, lack of acceptance, or lack of support

- **Security** - physical vulnerability, financial instability, or social intolerance

3.5 Do *you* have 'relational' competence?

"Do I have what?"

If so, *you* have a talent for and are comfortable with initiating and maintaining relationships of all types. *You* are comfortable with *personal disclosure* (section 3.1). Said another way, *you* can and will allow others to get to know the real you. *You* are comfortable with asserting displeasure or with expressing hurts; and, *you* do not hesitate to stand up for yourself or others.

Additionally, *you* are very comfortable with and capable of providing emotional support and advice and with showing genuine concern. *You* are able to manage interpersonal conflicts by: admitting when *you* are wrong, putting *your* own feelings aside when needed, and resolving a conflict fairly.

You intentionally avoid absolutes and having to resort to words like 'always' and 'never.' Those in healthy romantic or intimate relationships have most likely learned to identify and to speak what relationship expert and noted author Gary Chapman calls 'the five love languages'.

Finally. *You* are socially sensitive; a trait evidenced by *your* ability to be respectful of another's point of view and their associated feelings. Different than most, *you* care about *their* comfort as well as how *you* are perceived.

You never feel the need to have the **last** word.

3.6   'Attachment' styles *'yours and theirs'*

What's *your* relationship attachment style?

Attachment is a special emotional relationship that involves an exchange of comfort, care and/or pleasure. Attachment is also an important part of romantic love, so *our* attachment styles can have an impact on the health and the balance found in *our* relationships.

John Bowlby was a British psychological researcher in the 1950s and 60s who pioneered the study of attachment, separation, and loss. He found that - as children - we feel good about ourselves and our world if we have trustworthy adults that we can turn to. Many people have grown up without a secure base and can attest to how this has always made them unhappy, insecure, and unable to maintain satisfying relationships.

Everyone demonstrates an attachment style, which is a fusion of *their* experience as a child, *their* family attachment patterns, *their* personality, and *their* preferences. There are <u>four</u> different styles of attachment:

- **Secure**
- **Avoidant**

- **Anxious**
- **ambivalent**

What is *your* 'attachment' style? The 29-question personality quiz that follows is based upon several different assessment instruments developed and used by attachment researchers, including Hazen & Shaver (1987), Bartholomew & Horowitz (1991), and Brennan et al. (1998). These questions are not scored. Circling y*our* <u>honest</u> answers to each question can help *you* begin to determine *your* attachment style.

1. It's easy for me to be affectionate with my partner.

   - Neutral/Mixed

   - Disagree

   - Agree

2. I feel that my partner truly understands me.

   - Neutral/Mixed
   - Disagree
   - Agree

3. I don't worry about my partner abandoning me.

   - Neutral/Mixed

   - Disagree

   - Agree

4. I feel uncomfortable when my romantic partners reveal their emotions.

   - Neutral/mixed

   - Disagree

   - Agree

5. I find it easy to get close to romantic partners.

- Neutral/Mixed

- Disagree

- Agree

6. I can talk to my partner about my problems and concerns.

- Neutral/Mixed

- Disagree

- Agree

7. My romantic relationships are often shallow and lack real intimacy.

- Neutral/Mixed

- Disagree

- Agree

8. I am comfortable relying on romantic partners.

- Neutral/Mixed

- Disagree

- Agree

9. I am confident in feeling that my romantic partner cares for me.

- Neutral/Mixed

- Disagree

- Agree

10. I feel uncomfortable getting too close to romantic partners.

- Neutral/Mixed

- Disagree

- Agree

11. I get nervous when partners get too close.

- Neutral/Mixed

- Disagree

- Agree

12. I worry that my romantic partner does not feel as strongly about me as I do about him/her.

- Neutral/Mixed

- Disagree

- Agree

13. I find it difficult to depend on romantic partners.

- Neutral/Mixed

- Disagree

- Agree

14. I pull away when a romantic partner tries to get too close.

- Neutral/Mixed
- Disagree
- Agree

15. I feel uncomfortable sharing my thoughts or feelings with romantic partners.

- Neutral/Mixed
- Disagree
- Agree

16. I find it difficult to trust romantic partners.

- Neutral/Mixed
- Disagree
- Agree

17. I can go to my partner in times of stress.

- Neutral/Mixed
- Disagree
- Agree

18. I often make excuses to avoid spending time with romantic partners.

- Neutral/Mixed
- Disagree
- Agree

19. I can share my feelings and thoughts with my partner.

- Neutral/Mixed

- Disagree

- Agree

20. I prefer to be in a romantic relationship than not be in one.

- Neutral/Mixed

- Disagree

- Agree

21. I want to be very close to my romantic partners - this desire to be very close sometimes scares them away.

- Neutral/Mixed

- Disagree

- Agree

22. My partner understands my emotional needs.

- Neutral/Mixed

- Disagree

- Agree

23. My romantic partners do not want to get as close as I would like.

- Neutral/Mixed

- Disagree

- Agree

24. I spend a great deal of time worrying about my romantic relationships.

- Neutral/Mixed

- Disagree

- Agree

25. I prefer not to share my deep down feelings with a partner.

- Neutral/Mixed

- Disagree

- Agree

26. When I am not with my partner, I worry that he/she may be interested in somebody else.

- Neutral/Mixed

- Disagree

- Agree

27. I often worry that my partner will leave me.

- Neutral/Mixed

- Disagree

- Agree

28. If my romantic partner is not around when I need him/her, I become frustrated.

- Neutral/Mixed

- Disagree

- Agree

29. I worry that once my partner gets to really know me, he/she will no longer love me.

- Neutral/Mixed

- Disagree

- Agree

3.6.1

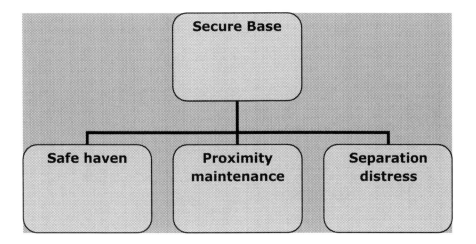

Characteristics of Attachment

There are <u>four</u> distinguishing characteristics of attachment:

Secure Base - The attachment figure acts as a base of security from which we can explore the surrounding environment.

Safe Haven - Returning to the attachment figure for comfort and safety in the face of a fear or threat.

Proximity Maintenance - The desire to be near the people we are attached to.

Separation Distress - Anxiety that occurs in the absence of the attachment figure.

3.6.2

Characteristics of <u>Secure</u> Attachment

As Children	As Adults
1. Able to separate from parents	2. Have trusting, lasting relationships
3. Seek comfort from parents when frightened	4. Tend to have good self-esteem
5. Return of parents is met with positive emotions	6. Comfortable sharing feelings with friends and partners
7. Prefers parents to strangers	8. Seeks out social support

Those with a **secure** attachment style tend to have good 'relational competence' and are comfortable making deposits into the 'emotional bank account' of others.

3.6.3

Characteristics of <u>Ambivalent</u> Attachment

As Children	As Adults
1. May be wary of strangers	2. Reluctant to become close to others
3. Become greatly distressed when the parent leaves	4. Worry that their partner does not love them
5. Do not appear to be comforted by the return of the parent	6. Become very distraught when a relationship ends

The **ambivalent** attachment style finds it difficult to invest emotionally, tends to see *their* relationships in shades of gray, and often uses <u>control dramas</u> like the 'interrogator', the 'aloof', or the 'poor me' to manipulate *their* partners.

3.6.4

Characteristics of <u>Avoidant</u> Attachment

As Children	As Adults
1. May avoid parents	2. May have problems with intimacy
3. Does not seek much comfort or contact from parents	4. Invests little emotion in social and romantic relationships
5. Shows little or no preference between parent and stranger	6. Unable or unwilling to share thoughts and feelings with others

Relationships go well when there is an underlying sense of trust, security, and stability. This, however, is not the perceived experience of the **avoidant**.

Unlike the avoidant, individuals who are secure in themselves are good at creating secure relationships. They help minimize - in others - any feelings of anxiety, distrust, hostility, and insecurity.

A wonderful companionship developed between **You** and **Me** as each had become increasingly more comfortable and intrigued with the others <u>social style</u> and <u>brands</u>. **You** shared with his new friend that he had struggled in previous relationships with understanding *his* role. He lost his mom at an early age

You and **Me**
on being *'authentic'*

and, subsequently, never quite let go of the grief and the sense of loss.

Me offered that she too struggled to find and maintain balance *(relational competence)* in her previous relationships and, consequently, was never quite certain as to what was expected of *her* regardless of whether it was family, work, or romance.

Me enjoyed immensely the easy <u>rapport</u> that she found with **You**. They were both easy-going music and art aficionados who also shared an equal love of pets and plants.

The two agreed - buoyed by a mutual feeling of trust and respect - to share those important aspects of themselves *(personal disclosure)* that they were reluctant or afraid to reveal to others.

You *(winking)* quipped … *"I'll show you my prized marble collection if you'll show me your magic box of cat whiskers!"* **Me** rolled with laughter.

友谊

"I present myself to you in a form suitable to the relationship I wish to achieve with you."

Luigi Pirandello

The fourth step: Acquaintances *'our pre-friends'*

Definition: someone you know a little, who is not a close friend; a relationship less intimate than friendship

Steven R. Covey, in *'The 7 habits of highly effective people'*, suggests that we *"begin with the end in mind."* It is a proactive statement of both vision and of personal responsibility. Begin each day with intent; give it direction, a destination and an outcome.

Acquaintances, new and familiar, are usually a part of each day's journey. When encountering an acquaintance such as: your mailman, your co-worker, your landlord, or your babysitter, do not hesitate to engage them sincerely. Understanding that few acquaintances will likely evolve into friendships, *you* can reduce or avoid awkward social tension and apprehension by allowing rapport - the naturally occurring seed of healthy communication - to grow of its own accord. Acquaintanceship can be a <u>static</u> type of relation remaining something just short of a <u>valued</u> friendship for years unless clear, deliberate, and repeated attempts are made at building on the perception of rapport.

> *"Remember that every good friend was once a stranger."*
>
> Anonymous

4.1   Who are 'they'?

- Co-workers
- classmates
- club members
- church members
- competitors
- neighbors

- service providers
- teachers
- coaches
- counselors
- distant relatives
- friends of friends

4.2   What do 'they' want? *'The short answer'*

- <u>Men</u>

  Trust, acceptance, appreciation, admiration, approval, and encouragement

- <u>Women</u>

  Caring, understanding, respect, devotion, validation, and   reassurance

Dr. John Gray, in his best-selling book *'Men are from Mars, Women are from Venus,'* makes it abundantly clear that men and women have similar but differing wants and needs and speak similar but differing languages. Successful acquaintanceships - like relationships - depend on *your* deliberate attempts and *your* versatile ability to communicate.

The most important component of this deliberate communication is listening to <u>understand</u>. Taking the time to reassure others that *we* not only hear *their* words but that *we* also understand *their* intent requires real effort and shows great patience, sincere interest, and unsolicited respect.

Dr. Gray also reminds *us* that we - men and women - are supposed to be different. *We* cannot expect that others can know or respond to our needs, desires, fears, or ambitions unless *we* are able to share them clearly. Neither can *we* get to know others unless *we* invite them to share *their* thoughts and feelings as *we* take the time to listen and understand without judging.

Lastly. Bishop T. D. Jakes, in his book *'He-motions'*, warns *us* to steer clear of **friend replacements**. These are imaginary relationships we establish with predictable and manageable: roles, jobs, activities, and responsibilities instead of with *people* who can potentially make us feel vulnerable and who are perceived as a source of future disappointment or hurt.

4.3   How do *you* turn 'acquaintanceship' into friendship?

#1   Be proactive

Definition: taking the initiative

Don't wait for others to take the initiative. Suggest and create opportunities to interact and to *'friend'* (section 4.4).

Practice mingling even if *you* do not feel particularly comfortable or adept at it. Parties, night clubs, church socials, wine tastings, film festivals, art shows, cultural festivals, music venues, karaoke bars, book clubs, sporting events, charity balls, silent auctions, weddings, day trips, and social clubs offer great opportunities to begin evolving acquaintanceships into potential friendships.

Seek first to understand, and then to be understood. Keep this top-of-mind as rapport begins to kindle with acquaintances. Trust that there will be plenty of time to talk about 'you'. Take the time early on to ask and learn about 'them'. Listening and learning will help *you* to avoid a poor investment of time and energy in someone with whom *you* may have very little in common.

#2   Be yourself

Definition: *in your normal state of body or mind*

You don't have to share everything but *you* do have to be sincere and honest about what *you* do share. Try avoiding premature expectations and relax *your* inhibitions. Be bold! Laugh easily, smile often, offer compliments when appropriate, and wear *your* brand(s) (section 2.2) proudly. Try walking a little further each time without the emotional, intellectual, material, social, spiritual, and physical crutches that tend to limit *our* friending efforts.

#3   Be patient

Definition: *showing the ability to endure or persevere*

Real and lasting rapport is discovered and not manufactured. Let the natural affinity - if it exists - flow and grow within the moment, the event, or the occasion. Remember that whatever *you* and *your* acquaintance have planned to do should be - first and foremost - fun!

Don't feel pressured by an acquaintance or create an expectation that a burgeoning friendship needs to be consummated in one day. It is likely to take several more interactions to determine if a mutual rapport truly exists. Finally; There are no <u>expiration</u> dates or <u>limited</u> time offers on 'real' friendship so don't feel slighted or offended if an acquaintance moves at a slower *friending* pace.

#4   Be consistent

<u>Definition:</u> *compatible; constant; unchanging*

Making deliberate and consistent attempts to communicate beyond the *incidental* and the *cordial* is very important. Sincere inquiries and a genuine interest in the lives of others will reveal that *you* can be selfless, supportive, and compassionate; the cornerstones of a meaningful friendship.

4.4   What is 'friending'?

Friending is the <u>deliberate</u> act of *cultivating* new and *maintaining* existing acquaintanceships and friendships. It is comprised of and identifiable by both *your* <u>active</u> and *your* <u>passive</u> behaviors and relies heavily upon *your* understanding of the following:

- social styles
- temperaments
- control dramas

- rapport types
- attachment styles
- introverts and extroverts

Friending is character-driven and its basic rules and skills are born from *your* **P. O. S.**; it is fueled or floundered by *your* <u>internal</u> goodwill and by *your* <u>external</u> efforts to establish rapport.

Each time *you* engage someone with warmth and sincerity - no matter the length of time or the method - *you* are being 'friendly' and are practicing the art of <u>active</u> *friending*.

Examples of <u>active</u> *friending* include:

- initiating a hello to a passerby
- initiating a brief and friendly chat with a coworker
- sending a thoughtful, warm, or funny text message or email to a loved one

- delivering a congratulations, sympathy, or get well card to a neighbor

- offering a timely and sincere explanation or apology to a disappointed friend

Examples of <u>passive</u> *friending* include:

- the return of an uninitiated, smile, hello, or wave from a neighbor or passerby

- taking or making the time to listen when engaged directly or by phone

- offering support and advice to a friend in a time of need

- receiving compliments or gifts graciously; and,

- withholding judgment or comment on a very sensitive matter

To guide *you* in becoming more 'friendly', there are ten *golden* rules in the next section that should be observed at <u>all</u> times and for <u>all</u> relationship conditions.

4.5   The ten 'golden rules' of friending:

I think that *we* would all agree - and history has repeatedly shown us - that without order, there is usually chaos. *Our* relationships are merely a microcosm of *our* larger society and function best when there are mutually respected rules.

While there are punitive laws to chasten *our* individual as well as collective societal behaviors, let *us* make sure that *we* always observe the following ten personal **rules of conduct** within *our* various relationship conditions.

1. Be responsive	6. Be helpful
2. Be sincere	7. Be flexible
3. Be on time	8. Be courteous
4. Be patient	9. Be trustworthy
5. Be respectful	10. Be selfless

Friending - in a nutshell - is a product of *your* **P. O. S.** (section 2.1) and the best external evidence of *your* character, *your* ethics, and *your* values.

Respecting and adhering to these golden rules ensures that *your* respective social styles (section 2.4) are able to '*walk your talk*'.

4.6   What is an 'emotional' bank account?

"we all have at least one!"

As *our* acquaintanceships evolve into friendships, *we* begin to accrue a measure of trust into an **emotional bank account**. That account grows when there are regular deposits of courtesy, honesty, kindness, thoughtfulness, patience, and consistency. When that account balance is high, *you* feel valued and secure; communication is easy and effective and *we* are more easily able to offer patience and the *benefit of the doubt* should a momentary 'trust' concern arise.

Whether *we* are cognizant of it or not, an *emotional* bank account exists for each of *our* relationship partners and relationship conditions regardless of whether they are friends, co-workers, or family. Some accounts overflow with abundant deposits from *'givers'* while others have minimum deposits or are often overdrawn by 'takers'. While *you* cannot control the behavior of others, *you* can manage *your* own deposits into the accounts of those in *your* relationship cycle (section 5.1).

If *you* value *your* relationships, do not neglect *your* accounts. Take the time and the initiative to frequently validate those relationships with unscripted and unsolicited sharing and caring. Don't wait to be asked or cajoled. Make a deposit regularly. They really do accrue interest.

It should be cautioned that investing heavily into an account that cannot be accessed *(usually the takers)* when needed is unwise. Emotional bank accounts should be as accessible as *your* personal checking account and NOT like a retirement account or a CD *(certificate of deposit)* which cannot be relied upon to be available when truly needed without suffering a penalty.

4.7   Are *'we'* friends?   *"really?"*

When does true friendship actually begin? The answer is subjective at best from one culture to another; but, it always seems to contain the same common denominators of: shared interests, likeability, loyalty, rapport, trust, selflessness, and acceptance.

If *you* are to consider yourself a 'true' friend or to be a part of a 'deep' friendship, *you* must exhibit a willingness to offer companionship, to accept and/or overlook another's minor faults, to support *their* interests, to offer and accept wise and timely counsel, and to safe guard each other's confidences.

One of the best indications that an acquaintanceship is evolving into a friendship is when unprompted words are spoken or when actions are taken that are meaningful, selfless, inclusive, and supportive. As a reference, here are the six qualities that best-selling author Dr. Barbara De Angelis – in her book *'Are you the one for me'* - suggests that *you* look for in a real friend or partner:

1. Commitment to personal growth

2. Emotional openness

3. Integrity

4. Maturity and responsibility

5. High self-esteem

6. Positive attitude toward life

A few months after the New Years eve party, **Him** unexpectedly invited **Me** out to dinner. Despite her continued attraction, she respectfully declined the invitation. The developing of a what felt like a genuine friendship with **You** made her all the more determined to reconcile her relationship cycle and keep the 'on-again off again'

You and **Me**
on *acquaintances &*
friending

interactions with **Him** as nothing more than the flirtations of a comfortable acquaintanceship.

Going back to their very first meeting as college freshmen, there had never honestly been quite enough rapport or enough common interests between **Me** and **Him** to justify anything more. **Me** often felt compelled to take the awkward initiative *(proactive friending)* of developing a genuine friendship but found **Him** continually lacking in a reciprocated interest, sincerity or follow through.

The pleasantly unexpected yet easy and affable rapport experienced with **You** on the night of the party awakened **Me** to a greater cognizance of the importance of good *friending*. She reasoned that taking the responsibility and the time to be proactive, to be responsive, to be respectful, to be flexible, and to have a sincere interest in others was paramount to any healthy relationship.

Me - happily - realized that she had in fact been developing a real friendship with **You**. He accepted her as she was and made her feel safe and important. Her emotional bank account grew each time that **You** kept his promises, listened with interest or did something with utter selflessness.

友谊

"The best mirror is an old friend."

Anonymous

Part III The relationship 'cycle'

The fifth step: The relationship 'cycle'

Definition: an interval during which a recurring sequence of events occurs; a periodically repeated sequence of events

5.1 What is it? *"it's definitely not linear!"*

The relationship *cycle* is the continual movement of acquaintances and family into and through three possible relationship <u>conditions</u> (section 1.0): *friendship*, *companionship,* and *partnership. Your* cycle, depending on *your* **P. O. S.** (section 2.1), and on *your* social versatility, can be very dynamic or virtually static. Rapport - vital to any new relationship - is the engine that puts *your* cycle into motion. The higher the sense of rapport, the higher the level of trust, and, subsequently, the further *you* will - ultimately - advance an acquaintance into *your* cycle. The healthy cycle continually encourages those within it to return to the principles that are the foundation of the friendship condition.

5.2 How does it work? *"it's really not complicated"*

Each of *us* - above the age of six - who is able and willing to communicate with immediate family, neighbors, and the outside world, has entered into some form of a relationship cycle. Family, for most of *us*, represents *our* first real opportunity to establish a relationship with someone of a differing social styles (section 2.4).

Depending on *your* immediate family structure, friendship and companionship tend to be cultivated by the examples dsiplayed by *our* elders and are reinforced in *our* early education. As *our* communcation portals (section 3.3) develop and *we* mature, *we* are better able to engage outsiders and better able to share *our* broader interests, our passions, and our experiences.

Acquaintances -for the purposes of explaining the relationship cycle - represent any moderately familiar family member, co-worker, classmate, team member, neighbor, or service provider. It is a given that the vast majority of *our* acquaintances will <u>never</u> become actual friends. Those who do, have - through deliberate friending behaviors - established a level of rapport and a sufficient measure of trust. Thus, the cycle begins. Rapport grows and, in cases where it is coupled with physical attraction and/or shared interests, friendship can evolve into companionship. Companionships can be either platonic or intimate, and - depending on mutual needs/desires - evolve into partnerships. For the sake of clarity, it must be stated that neither physical attraction nor romantic interest is necessary to form friendships, companionships or partnerships.

Further; when someone enters into *your* <u>relationship cycle</u>, it is seldom to play a 'fixed' role. Trust, distance, needs, personal events, and time continually pull relationships in one direction or another. The healthy cycle is the one that - despite its current condition – is balanced and appreciates that friendship is the key to all relationship successes.

5.3 What are 'gray' areas? *"are they complicated?"*

> Definition: *an intermediate area; a topic that is not clearly one thing or the other; an undefined situation or subject that does not seem to conform to known categories or rules*

If *you* have seen the movie *'it's complicated'* starring Meryl Streep and Alec Baldwin, *you* will have at least a humorous idea of what is meant by gray areas.

Jane and Jake - a divorced but still friendly middle-aged couple of twenty years - discover that they still have deep feelings for each other. They reignite a passionate - albeit unwise - love affair. The chemistry and attraction that brought them together thirty years earlier was still very much alive as was a surprising and newly found appreciation for each others evolving social style and brands. Absent where most of the inhibitions, denials and filtering that sabotaged their once-envied marriage.

Jake - now married ten years to his former mistress - is so genuinely convicted by his renewed feelings that he begins to secretly and yet aggressively pursue Jane. Within weeks, he makes plans to leave his hot young wife. Jane - single but casually dating her architect - is conflicted by the guilt of playing a part in her ex's new infidelity. She feels moderately validated by Jakes earnest and unrelenting courtship.

Unable to cope with the *gray* area created by her re-emerging feelings for Jake and the unanticipated affection for her new Architect, Jane ends the ill-fated affair. Her solution? **Reconcile!** (section 5.5) Jane chose to put into balance her full relationship cycle - her children, her business, her ex and her friends - by limiting her wonderful and undeniable bond with Jake to a platonic friendship. Dissapointed, Jake listened and ultimately respected the concerns and the needs of his ex-wife and, subsequently, valued their enduring friendship all the more.

Gray areas in relationships are common. Seldom do *we* meet someone of interest who is completely unencumbered. Gray areas describe overlapping or unresolved relationship conditions and involments that cannot be defined by a single category. The causes can be ideological, spiritual, physical, and emotional. Sometimes *our* most difficult struggles have been in trying to define in *'black and white'* terms something that may always be gray. Accepting the occassional *gray* areas - those without condition or promise - can be liberating and empowering for some. The pressure to define, shape or control a relationship can potentially destroy it.

To accept that previous likes and loves can occassionally bleed into new likes and loves, does not mean, however, that *you* are not responsible for *your* choices and *your* actions. Honesty is still paramount. If *you* are dating someone new and yet still have feelings for an ex, *your* unambiguous disclosure will aid the new friend in determining how involved *they* may want to become. Speaking *your* truth benefits both *you* and those around *you*. They will respect *your* honesty even if *they* are dissapointed that *you* are not able to invite *their* full interest.

The following are **six** factors that contribute to the reasons why gray areas persist in *our* lives:

1. *We* are still getting over a previous relationship

2. The perception that *others* have too much baggage

3. *We* are afraid of rejection

4. *We* are afraid of settling and/or commitment

5. *We* don't feel good about *ourselves*

6. *We* don't want to give up *our* freedom

Simply put; *gray* areas are a constant whether *you* acknowledge them or not. Many entering new relationships unwisely try to manage them by forcing their new partner to completely disclose,

73

disavow, or disassociate with old friends, partners or activities. Unless trust has been broken, this is an unacceptable condition of a new friendship.

Manage *your* gray areas with integrity and transparency so that *others* will not feel the need to.

5.4   What is 'plotting'?   *"does it help?"*

Definition: *to mark or note on as if on a map or chart*

FRIENDS FIRST uses the exercise of plotting as a means of helping *you* visualize *your* existing relationship cycle.

Plotting allows *you* to see how many acquaintances, friends, companions and partners are currently orbiting in *your* social solar system.

On the pages that follow are some examples of Relationship cycles. A blank cycle is offered at the end of this section for *your* personal use. Plot by filling in the three relationship condition boxes as well as the acquaintanceship box as best you can.

You don't need full names for this exercise but *you* do need to be honest; especially regarding the gray areas. Place an asterisk next to any names that may represent a gray area for *you*.

With *your* clear understanding of the differences between the relationship conditions of *friend, companion,* and *partner* (section 1.0), *you* can now evaluate and - hopefully - better appreciate those who make up *your* existing relationship cycle. *You* can also see - from *your* acquaintanceship box - the potential *(or the lack of it)* for new friendships.

What is the most important <u>function</u>, and, subsequently, the biggest <u>benefit</u> of looking at *your* relationship 'cycle' and <u>plotting</u> honestly what *you* see?

The answer? **Reconciling!**

5.5 What is 'reconciling'? *"...and why is it necessary?"*

<u>Definition:</u> *bringing into harmony; to reestablish a close relationship; to settle or resolve*

Successful <u>reconciling</u> in relationships is the art of managing the *wrong* things the *right* way.

Now that *you* have plotted *your* current relationships and acquaintanceships, the next important step is to reconcile *your* *relationship cycle.* "What exactly does this mean? and; why should *you* do it?"

<u>Reconciling</u> allows *you* to look closely at those persons listed in each category as well as its related <u>gray</u> area to see if the relationship condition is <u>accurate,</u> <u>emotionally healthy,</u> and <u>appropriate</u>. Reconciling can mean: reviving old, confirming good, growing new, and - when justified - <u>retiring</u> relationships.

For example. If *you* have just committed to be exclusive partners to someone but are continuing to pursue or allow a romantic dialogue and encounters with another, *you* would be wise to reconcile the non-committed romantic daliance back to a platonic friendship or avoid making a new commitment of exclusivity that *you* cannot keep.

If *you* have developed a platonic friendsip into an intimate companionship whose partner now demands that *you* no longer engage *your* other friends socially, strongly consider reconciling that new intimate companionship back to a platonic friendship. *Your* existing, healthy, and valued friendships should NOT be sacrificed for the sake of a new and more demanding relationship condition.

Ultimately, the exercise of reconciling is one of proactive and responsible relationship management; a veritable balancing of *your* various emotional bank accounts (section 4.6). Each of us has - at one time or another - done too little or allowed too much. Reconciling is not an opportunity to try to change *others*, to present ultimatums, or to be punative; instead, it is an opportunity to change or better *your* particular friending behaviors. If the various relationships in *your* cycle are rooted in an abiding friendship based on trust and respect, very little needs to be done.

For those friendships whose foundations have crumbled but can be rebuilt over time, take the bold initiative to address the problems and suggest solutions. If an amicable solution cannot be found or is not desired, push the '*enough'* button. *You* have likely outgrown the relationship condition and need to retire it without ill will. That energy is better expended on building new friendships and on investing more time and energy in existing healthy ones.

On the following pages are several examples of relationship cycles. Make a copy of the blank cycle provided; take the time to plot *your* current relationship conditions honestly and accurately. Don't forget the gray areas!

"Do any of your 'conditions' need to be reconciled?"

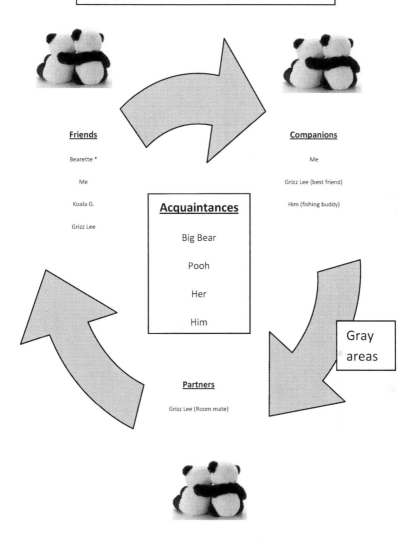

The relationship cycle

Friends

Bearette *

Me

Koala G.

Grizz Lee

Companions

Me

Grizz Lee (best friend)

Him (fishing buddy)

Acquaintances

Big Bear

Pooh

Her

Him

Gray areas

Partners

Grizz Lee (Room mate)

Sample relationship cycle for: You

<u>Note:</u> Asterisk (*) indicates a gray area (ex-girlfriend)

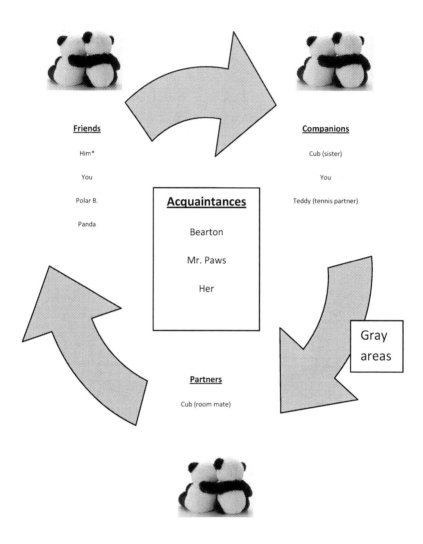

The relationship cycle

Friends

Him*

You

Polar B.

Panda

Companions

Cub (sister)

You

Teddy (tennis partner)

Acquaintances

Bearton

Mr. Paws

Her

Gray areas

Partners

Cub (room mate)

Sample relationship cycle for: Me

<u>Note:</u> Asterisk (*) indicates a gray area (casually dating)

The relationship cycle

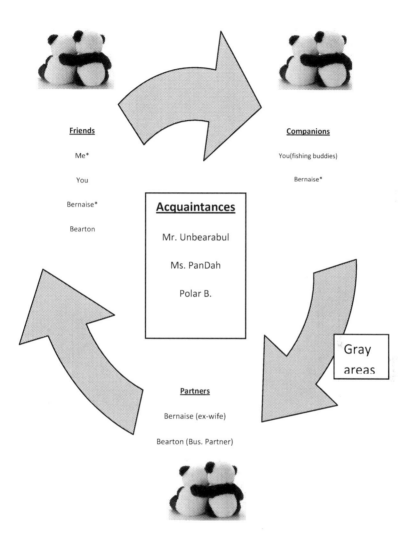

Friends

Me*

You

Bernaise*

Bearton

Companions

You(fishing buddies)

Bernaise*

Acquaintances

Mr. Unbearabul

Ms. PanDah

Polar B.

Gray areas

Partners

Bernaise (ex-wife)

Bearton (Bus. Partner)

Sample relationship cycle for: Him

Note: Asterisk (*) indicates a gray area (casually dating), (ex-wife)

Your relationship cycle

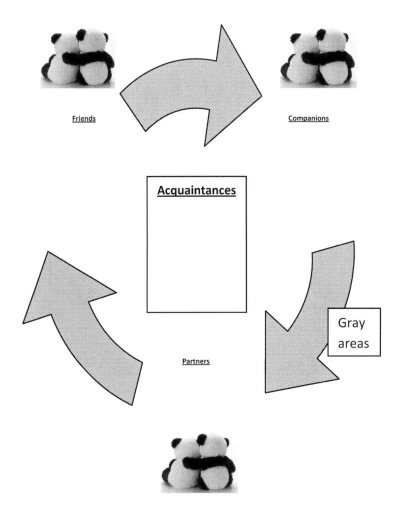

Friends

Companions

Acquaintances

Gray areas

Partners

Sample relationship cycle for: _____

You laughed heartily upon hearing the news that **Me** had so boldly reconciled her <u>relationship cycle</u> with **Him**. She had successfully- if not reluctantly - moved a once-romantic <u>companionship</u> back to a platonic <u>acquaintanceship</u>.

You and **Me**
on *relationship cycles*

"Bravo!" exclaimed a sincerely supportive **You**. *"That kind of change is almost always easier said than done."*

Me exhaled and smiled with great personal satisfaction. For as far back as she could remember, she had repeatedly allowed unhealthy interests and relationships to linger until they ultimately became toxic. Too often, there were instances of unresolved personal issues, social conflicts, or persistent communication miscues.

You seized this opportunity to share that recently he had recently taken a hard look at his various relationships and discovered a desperate need to do some <u>reconciling</u> of his own. He valued those that he considered his real friends but definitely needed to modify the context of some of his other relationships. **You** wanted to identify and to grow the healthy friendships that he could the confidently share with others in a productive and meaningful way.

You and **Me** understand that reconciling the <u>gray</u> areas in their respective <u>relationship cycles</u> should be done without being either ambiguous or punitive.

友谊

"Friendship with oneself is all-important because without it one cannot be friends with anyone else in the world."

Eleanor Roosevelt

Part IV   Discover *You,* Discover *Me*
part 2

The sixth step: *Your* P. O. S. 'part 2'

6.1   Are *you* willing to make changes?

Success in any endeavor requires a willingness to learn, to adapt and to grow. *You* are revisiting *your* **P. O. S.** (section 2.1) to determine what changes *you* want or need to make in order to better *your* <u>friending</u> and <u>relationship</u> habits.

You are a creature of habit governed by a particular ethic. As much as ninety-eight percent of what *you* do day-to-day is carried out as habit; and, while most habits are essential to accomplishing *your* goals and objectives, some can have a crippling effect on *your* life.

Steven R. Covey, in his book '*The 7 habits of highly effective people*', identifies two success ethics found in our culture. The first and the oldest is called the ***character*** ethic. The second - developed over the last sixty years - is called the ***personality*** ethic.

Success literature in this country and abroad - going back hundreds of years - was grounded in principles like: integrity, fidelity, humility, temperance, justice, courage, patience, industry, modesty, and simplicity. These are the foundational values of the *character* ethic. They are universal and easily understood even if they are sometimes difficult to live up to. These values offer a great barometer for those desiring to divine the worthy from the not-so-worthy for: leadership, matrimony, credit, education, or employment.

In the last half century, a new approach to success and relationship building emerged centering on *our* personas. It followed two paths: The first was human and public; the second was P̲ositive M̲ental A̲ttitude or PMA. *Our* image and *our* ability to influence others became the call to action. It was the **personality** ethic and the birth of personal branding (section 2.2). Winning friends, influencing others, dressing for success, mastering rapport, power talking, attitude altering, and network building had pushed the *character* ethic into the passenger seat.

Building long-lasting and meaningful relationships demands that the **character** ethic re-take the drivers position in *our* social lives and that the *Personality* ethic plays a strong supporting role.

6.2 What are *your* 'must haves' in <u>any</u> relationship condition?

Whether *you* are a friend, a companion, or a partner, there are always **must haves** or **deal breakers**. Stated or understood, there are levels of expectation within each <u>relationship condition</u> (section 1.0). It is wise to share these <u>must haves</u> and <u>deal breakers</u> with those in a **partnership** condition early on as they are established within and, thusly, supported by *your* **P. O. S.**

Your value within and *your* respect for a particular relationship will be determined by an observance of these <u>MHs</u> and <u>DBs</u>. Some common examples are listed below.

Circle the examples below that best represent *your* needs.

1. Trust
2. honesty
3. respect
4. accountability
5. integrity
6. ambition
7. humility
8. self-discipline
9. sense of humor
10. financial stability
11. advanced education

12. religious
13. spiritual
14. liberal
15. conservative
16. tolerance
17. forgiving
18. family-oriented
19. adventurous
20. socially competent
21. athletic
22. culturally compatible

6.2.1 The six biggest 'mistakes' *we* make

Definition: an incorrect idea, judgment, choice, or opinion

A sense of balance in a healthy relationship is experienced if <u>must haves</u> are identified and respected early, and, subsequently are reciprocated by *you* as <u>must dos</u>. *You* should be able to give what *you* expect to receive without prompt or condition.

The following is a list of the six **biggest** mistakes that *we* make in the beginning of *our* relationships according to Dr. Barbara De Angelis in her best-seller *'Are you the one for me?'*

1. *We* don't ask enough questions.

2. *We* ignore warning signs of potential problems.

3. *We* make premature compromises.

4. *We* give in to 'lust blindness'.

5. *We* give in to material seduction.

6. *We* put commitment before compatibility.

Your (new or improved) **relationship mantra:**

Ask relevant and but tactful questions; be wary and be decisive regarding any obvious warning signs; avoid unnecessary compromises; resist the powerful seduction of physical lust and of material branding; and, make social and personal compatibility and not the 'idea' of commitment the ultimate goal.

6.3 Social paradigm shifts *"be ready for change"*

Social paradigms are models of behavior *you* have either been taught or have learned to follow - through emulation or imitation - as a means of getting along with others. When someone says something like: *"well, that's just the way I am"*, they are expressing a <u>current</u> and a <u>particular</u> type of behavior.

To successfully manage all of *your* <u>relationship conditions</u>, *you* may have to seriously consider making a behavioral shift. For example: If normal to *you* is to be negative and pessimistic, but *you* have friends who are positive and optimistic, rapport *(comfortable and desirable communication and companionship)* will suffer or be completely lost unless *you* are willing and able to make changes.

A commonly accepted principle in any desired behavioral change is that a significant *'breakthrough'* requires a significant *'break with'* old habits. Thus, success in the quality of *your* relationships will greatly depend on *your* ability to be both <u>socially versatile</u> (section 2.4) and to <u>change</u> certain kinds of behaviors or expectations.

If *you* are typically <u>reactive</u> in *your* social style versus <u>proactive</u>, *you* may have become fixed and comfortable in a posture that expects others to engage *you* first; others are expected to: please *you*, soothe *you*, appease *you*, seek *your* approval or forgiveness, subordinate *their* needs, and initiate all activities. When *they* do not take the initiative, learned defensive behaviors may lead *you* to potentially see *them* as aloof, self-centered, arrogant, selfish, unworthy, disloyal, or anti-social.

Shyness, a fear of rejection, a sense of entitlement, control issues, and previous relationship failures are the likely causes of this type of posturing. To counter <u>reactive</u> tendencies, practice being and doing what *you* have come to expect of others.

Dr. Wayne Dyer, in his book *'The power of intention'*, recommends that *you* remain in a state of eternal gratitude for everyone who has ever played a relationship role in *your* life; each having offered an insight into self and another opportunity for *you* to learn and to grow.

6.4   **N**euro-**A**ssociative **C**onditioning

Definition: *teach or accustom; a circumstance or state*

Anthony Robbins, peak performance coach and author of: *Awaken the giant within, Unlimited Power,* and the *Personal Power* tape series, offers another approach to changing or modifying *your* **P. O. S.** - for the better - through his personal science called **N**euro-**A**ssociative **C**onditioning (NAC).

NAC was developed by Robbins from the early works of: Neuro-linguistic Programming (NLP) founders Richard Bandler and Dr. John Grinder; the psychology and language strategies of Dr. Milton Erickson; and, the General Semantics (GS) philosophies of Alfred Korzybski.

Robbins describes the process of change in *you* and *I* as one based upon the premise that there are two determining reasons for all human behavior:

1.) The need to avoid pain **2.)** The desire to gain pleasure.

How does this relate to positively modifying *your* **P. O. S.** and successful relationship building? NAC suggests that *we* typically go through *our* daily lives acting or reacting based on pain/pleasure conditioning and the links that have *already* been established to this conditioning within *our* brains.

Examples:

Pain: conflict, public speaking, embarrassment, deadlines, exercise, rejection, failure, etc.

Pleasure: good food, approval, dancing, success, music, painting, reading, shopping, sex, etc.

If *you* find that *you* are apprehensive or even adverse to 'friending' and/or relationship building, *you* may already have some notions as to why: Past hurts or disappointments? Feelings of inadequacy? Fear of rejection? Unresolved emotional issues? Unrealistic expectations?

Better relationships can only be achieved with a better *you*. Don't let negative conditioning - formed by painful associations to past, present, or imagined future events - cripple or destroy *your* relationship cycle (section 5.1). Instead, Robbins implores *you* to start making new 'pleasurable' associations. Imagine and then anticipate the feelings of acceptance and validation that *you* would like to experience in *your* various relationship conditions and then take positive and meaningful new actions.

6.5 'Emotional' intelligence: *"do you have it?"*

Dr. Daniel Goleman, in his book *'Emotional intelligence: why it can matter more than IQ'*, proffers that *our* emotional IQ - comprised of self-awareness, impulse control, persistence, zeal, self-motivation, empathy, and social deftness - is the part of human intelligence that can matter most in how successfully *we* deal with relationships. These abilities are the hallmarks of character and self-discipline, and of altruism and compassion.

Dr. Goleman suggests that people with high emotional IQs flourish within intimate relationships, and are the stars within affinity groups, fraternal organizations, and the workplace. The lack of emotional intelligence can undermine relationships, sabotage careers, and even lead to poor physical health.

Emotional intelligence starts with being self-aware; which, in short, means being immediately cognizant of *your* particular mood and of *your* thoughts about that particular mood. Those who are acutely self-aware tend to be much better at managing their emotions, their actions, and tend to have a more positive outlook on life; they seldom ruminate or obsess and, as a result, are able to get *'back to good'* more quickly than others.

Self-awareness *(intrapersonal intelligence)* also allows *you* to continually develop two very important social competences in dealing with others *(interpersonal intelligence)*:

1.) self-management and **2.)** empathy.

These competences - common in effective leaders and relationship builders - then permit *you* to shape social encounters, to influence and inspire others, to thrive in intimate relationships, and to put others at ease.

Warmth, curiosity, respect, selflessness, and the ability to create boundaries are the desirable qualities of those with high emotional intelligence. The next step (section 6.6) will cover dealing with situations where *your* emotional intelligence can and will be put to the test.

6.6   Dealing with the emotions of *'others'*

"do we have to?"

Definition: *a strong feeling such as love, anger, joy, guilt, envy, or fear*

In his book *"Getting through to people"*, Dr. Jesse S. Nirenberg describes **emotion** essentially as a force that creates tension and, subsequently, motivates *us* to action. Dr. Nirenberg suggests that the most common and the most effective way of dealing with the tensions created by emotions is through verbal communication.

First. Understanding that humans - governed by both internal *(invisible)* and external *(visible)* factors - don't react to a given set of circumstances the exact same way, *you* should never presume another's emotional state. Asking a friend or acquaintance to express how *they* feel is usually the best place to start.

Second. Because *you* are not privy to the emotional inner life of another, it is best not to judge, trivialize, or reason away *their* emotional expressions or states. A person consumed with worry or fear, for example, is not always able to verbalize or rationalize just why *they* are feeling that particular emotion at that particular moment.

Third. Emotions are often displaced. According to Dr. Nirenberg, it is not uncommon for *us* to take out *our* anger or anxiety regarding one circumstance on someone or something barely related to the true source of the emotion. Displacing our emotions is actually an act of concealment. It is usually an attempt to shift and relieve a tension stemming from a conflict in *our* inner world to some person or object outside *ourselves*.

Finally. Since emotions can be displaced, logic is seldom effective in helping get rid of undesired emotional tension. *"Emotions simply are not responsive to reason"* according to Dr. Nirenberg.

Attempting to apply reason usually has the undesirable effect of making the other person feel irrational.

Here are <u>three</u> helpful ways to deal with the emotions of others:

1. **Encourage expression.** This helps relieve the tension created by the particular emotion. Be prepared to just listen. Do not rationalize or form judgments.

2. **Make the other person aware of *their* feelings.** *Our* emotions are a valuable part of *our* life experience. Do not assume the emotional state of another. *You* can share that *their* behavior seems to <u>indicate</u> a certain emotional state and that it is understandable. Ask *them* to verbalize what *they* are feeling.

3. **Accept emotions without offering criticism.** This is the foundation of genuine friendship. Accepting the various emotional states of another requires both patience and restraint. Unless there is imminent danger, or *you* are asked directly, keep opinions to *yourself*.

6.7 'Control' dramas: *"unfortunately, we've all used these"*

Question1: Have *you* ever uttered or heard someone else say something like this? *"I don't need the drama!"*

Each of us - as a result of *our* particular upbringing and *our* social conditioning - tends to manage *our* various relationships using one or more of four different <u>control dramas</u>:

Intimidators steal energy and control from others by means of threat. **Interrogators** steal energy and control by judging and questioning. **Aloofs** attract attention *(and energy)* to *themselves* and exercise indirect control by acting reserved, unavailable, or by withdrawing. **Poor me's** exercise *their* control by making *us* feel guilty and responsible for *them*.

The above descriptions most notably referenced in author James Redfield's best-seller, *'The Celestine Prophecy'*, define the four ways that people tend to be in relationship with one another. All four are attempts to control *another's* behavior.

Question 2: What is this need *we* have to control? And, Why do *we* feel it is necessary?

Answer: *We* attempt to control and to manipulate others because *we* believe that if *they* would change *their* behavior *we* would be happy and, subsequently, so would *they*. When people do things *we* don't like, or when *we* are not getting *our* way, *we* think *they* are wrong. Believing that *we* are right and that *they* are wrong, *we* then think that *we* have the right to impose *our* beliefs or needs on *them*. What *we* are attempting to do is to protect or secure *our* beliefs, *our* practices, or *our* comfort zones.

On the following page are some examples of the <u>tendencies</u> of each control drama.

The intimidator

- Uses: physical confrontation, subordination, verbal, emotional, and material threats

The interrogator

- Uses: criticism, negative word play, policing, and antagonistic questioning

The poor me

- Uses: emotion, guilt, charm, or physical actions for empathy or support

The aloof

- Uses physical and emotional distance; pulls away quickly, shuts down, or is not responsive; is guarded; is unavailable until appeased or made comfortable

Virtually all of *us* - regrettably - have employed at least one or more control dramas in the history of *our* personal, team, affinity, and employment relationships. Ultimately, they are unhealthy, ineffective, and are always destructive. These behaviors tend to leave *us* feeling frustrated, disappointed, unsupported and alone. Similarly, they leave *our* friends and relationship partners feeling distrustful, unappreciated, manipulated, unsettled, and exhausted.

<u>Recognize</u> *your* control dramas and <u>avoid</u> those of others.

Reconciling *our* relationship cycles is about assessing the 'value' of those *we* call *our* friends and determining whether or not *we* have placed them in the roles best

You and **Me**
on adjusting *your* **P. O. S.**

suited for *us*. Looking inward first, *we* reconnect to *our* own character, *our* values, and *our* ethics. There *we* find *our* must haves. **Me's** breakthrough with **Him** came when she realized that she finally had the courage to overcome the conditioned sense of loss or pain associated with what she perceived as failure. Fortunately for her, she didn't stop there. **Me** - the youngest and most introverted of four - reached out to her estranged siblings and began to heal the wounds of growing up in a dysfunctional family.

You talked often with her about how he had learned to rely on his emotional intelligence to get and to keep his life in balance. Recognizing that others can and will play on *his* emotions to satisfy *their* needs was an invaluable epiphany. **You** finally felt secure and, subsequently, empowered to encourage others to express themselves without feeling vulnerable or manipulated. Reconciling **Him** back to an acquaintanceship - while not easy - was a meaningful victory for **Me** over a particular control drama. **Him** was a classic aloof personality. He needed to be pursued, soothed and/or appeased and never gave more than was absolutely necessary. A relationship of any condition would always be on *his* terms; and, avoidance, limited communication or the complete withdrawal of affection were the tactics that he would use to get his way. **Me** could hardly believe that she had allowed herself to be manipulated in that way. Oddly enough, she actually began to feel sorry for others drawn in and manipulated by that type of control drama.

友谊

Kahlil Gibran

The seventh step: The pursuers and the pursued

Definition: who pursues or chases: one who follows in haste, with a view to overtake

7.1 'Managing' friends 'who want more'

From reactive to proactive

For many of *you*, there will be times when *you* will be forced to manage the expectations of friends or acquaintances who desire a relationship condition (section 1.0) or a level of engagement (section 1.4) that *you* do not. Unfortunately, there is not a realistic way to completely avoid these uncomfortable instances - typically born of a physical attraction, a feeling of rapport, or both - experienced exclusively by another.

If there is a 'relationship' line that *you* do not desire to cross and that *you* do not wish to have crossed by another, honesty, clarity, and consistency are of paramount importatnce in *your* verbal and non-verbal communication. It is very important that *you* allow *your* 'personal' truths (section 3.1) to work for *you*.

If, for example, an acquaintanceship or a platonic friendship is all that *you* desire, say so tactfully and do not - under any circumstance - send mixed signals. Appreciating that all worthwhile relationships are based in mutual respect, honesty and trust, deceit should never be employed to dissuade or to discourage. If *your* clearly 'stated' boundaries are not honored, respectfully and immediately <u>retire</u> (section 5.5) the relationship.

7.2   'Respecting' friends *'who do not want more'*

From proactive to reactive

Each of *us* can recall - at least once - the unpleasant experience of feeling 'smitten' or 'love-lorn' over an unreciprocated interest. A sign of *our* continuing maturity is displayed in how well *we* handle what can be tantamount to either indifference or rejection. The uncomfortable fact someone may not desire to bond with *us* is not evidence of *our* social shortcoming; rather, it is an uncomfortable reminder of the unpredictable and uncontrollable natures of attraction, rapport, and timing.

Socio-economic factors, cultural beliefs, fear, unresolved hurts, and existing commitments can also negatively skew a *friending* process and can leave *you* short of *your* desired relationship goal. <u>Accepting</u> and then immediately <u>honoring</u> *another's* social boundaries is a sign of maturity, respect, and prudence. Thank them sincerely for *their* candor; do not interrogate or cajole; and, do not allow momentary feelings of dissapointment to pull *you* out of character. Commit yourself fully to being cordial and gracious and to enjoying what gifts of <u>friending</u> *they* are <u>currently</u> comfortable in offering.

Despite his promise to respect **Me's** wishes, **Him** - unaccustomed to rejection - immediately began to employ the 'poor me' <u>control drama</u> in a self-serving attempt to win her over. Apologies quickly turned into charm-laced requests for work and personal favors. Unsolicited and often uncomfortable expressions of affection were also used as a desperate but ineffective play for empathy and understanding.

You and **Me**
on managing *unreciprocated interests*

Frustrated and annoyed, **Me** stayed true to her new resolve and followed **You's** timely advice to remain patient and to consistently remind **Him** that there are boundaries that she will no longer cross. If he could not respect those boundaries, she would have to consider his intentions a 'deal breaker' and will regrettably have to cease all communication by <u>retiring</u> the relationship.

Two months into her new resolve, **Him** tries once again to manipulate **Me's** feelings by offering to take her out on her birthday. She thanked him for both his thoughtfulness and his kind offer but respectfully declined this and any future invitations.

友谊

"All love that has not friendship for its base is like a mansion built upon the sand."

Ella Wheeler Wilcox

Part V   Let's look at *your* relationship 'cycle'...*again*!

The eighth step: Making the relationship 'pact'

8.1   The ten personal 'commitments':

There is little chance of developing good and healthy relationships if *you* cannot keep *your* own pacts and live by *your* own rules. Below is a list of commitments that each of *us* should honor in defense of *our* **P. O. S.** (section 2.1). These commitments help keep *us* from placing unwanted or unrealistic burdens upon *our* friends.

"I will...

take ownership of my relationships."

be socially versatile and adapt to other social styles."

accept being vulnerable."

be forthcoming and honest."

grow friendships whenever possible."

make others feel safe and valued."

always be civil and respectful."

not give ultimatums and not force change."

not quibble, interrogate, or be punitive."

not interfere in the relationships of others."

Take each of these statements to heart. Post them in a place where *you* will be constantly reminded and encouraged to live up to *your* pact.

8.2   The <u>ten</u> types of relationships that <u>fail</u>:

Just in case *your* **P. O. S.** did not already feature some (or all) of the 'commitments' in the previous section, they have been listed in the previous section as a reminder that *you* should always be aware of *your* role and *your* responsibilities in each of *your* various <u>relationship conditions</u> (section 1.0). The burden of greater care and civility is never shifted to others for *your* choices or *your* actions. Should *your* relationship(s) begin to falter, look first to the ten commitments in section 8.1.

Dr. Barbara De Angelis - in her best-seller *'Are you the one for me'* - reminds *us* that, while commitments of conduct are important within relationships, *we* must first be aware of the **ten types** of relationships that just <u>won't</u> work.

1. *You* care more about *your* partner than *he* or *she* cares about *you*.

2. *Your* partner cares more about *you* than *you* do about *him* or *her*.

3. *You* are in love with *your* partner's potential.

4. *You* are on a rescue mission.

5. *You* look up to *your* partner as a role model.

6. *You* are infatuated with *your* partner for external reasons.

7. *You* have only partial compatibility.

8. *You* choose a partner in order to be rebellious.

9. *You* choose a partner as a reaction to *your* previous partner.

10. *Your* partner is unavailable.

If *you* are in one of these types of relationships, 'reconcile' it as soon as possible back to a <u>healthy</u> and <u>balanced</u> condition. Do not make the mistake of thinking that an attempt at fixing the *other* person fixes the problem(s). *You*, and *you* alone, are responsible for the decisions and the actions that defend and/or support *your* emotional and relationship health.

8.3   **Stats** and **studies:**

The top fifteen relationship statistics <u>everyone</u> should know

1. **44%** of the adult population is single.

2. On average, there are **86** single men to every **100** single women in the U. S.

3. The **#1** relationship argument is over money.

4. Only **2%** of men and **9%** of women find relationships in bars and nightclubs.

5. **63%** of married couples claim to have found their mates through a network of friends.

6. **51%** percent of singles say that flattery is the best way to attract someone.

7. **88%** of women find money to be very important in a relationship.

8. **52%** of singles feel that they are too busy to meet other singles.

9. **80%** of men date women that are at least 5 years younger than they are.

10. **76%** of women date men that are at least 5 years older than they are.

11. **2%** of Americans get married every year.

12. According to the US Census bureau, there are close to 96 million unmarried people. **47%** are men. **53%** are women.

13. **61%** of adults have never been married. **24%** have divorced at least once.

14. **48%** of adults believe that a person can be happy without getting married.

15. **46%** of adults say that they would be happy living in a committed relationship indefinitely without getting married.

Note: These statistics change annually.

Sources: US Census Bureau; Pew Research/ Internet and American Life project; Sex in America: A definitive survey by Robert T. Michael; Who uses online dating; Unmarried and single Americans week; Trends of interracial dating and marriage; Eharmony; Match.com; Chemistry.com/Harris interactive

You and **Me**
on the *relationship pact*

New Year's eve. On their one year anniversary as companions and friends, **You** and **Me** decided to take the next step. The growth of their mutual emotional affection (section 1.5) had made them confident enough to evolve their relationship condition from friendship to partnership and their physical involvement (section 1.4) from platonic to romantic.

In the 12 months since first meeting, **You** and **Me** had come to understand and appreciate some very important things about each other:

You was a moderately extroverted 'driver' with a 'secure' attachment style who admitted to having occasionally employed the 'interrogator' control drama.

Me was an introverted 'amiable' with 'analytical' tendencies. She was learning to counter her 'anxious' attachment style, and when stressed, often employed the 'poor me' and the 'interrogator' control dramas. Continued relationship success was predicated on both growing their <u>relational competence</u> and living by an agreed upon pact.

Accepting that *they* were not PERFECTLY suited for each other and will probably always feel vulnerable in some way, they agreed to: take full ownership of *their* relationship, continue practicing socially versatile, be forthcoming and honest, continually grow *their* friendship, make each other feel safe and valued, always be civil and respectful, avoid ultimatums, avoid being punitive and avoid interfering in the relationships of others.

Now, when **You** and **Me** have the occasion to reflect on *their* cherished partnership, they are mindful that *their* individual <u>wants</u> are second to *their* sincere and mutual <u>need</u> to do what is in the best interest of *their* <u>friendship</u>.

友谊

Part VI   *Your* relationship 'toolbox'

The ninth step: More helpful 'tools'

What follows are a few question-and-answer tools to help *you* better determine *your* disposition regarding <u>friends</u> and <u>acquaintances</u>. These questions are not meant to be scientific and are offered only as a window into *your* current <u>friending</u> behaviors (section 4.4).

FRIENDSFIRST is neither written nor recommended as a tool to be used to modify or to fix *others;* rather, it is to be used as a guide to help address, adjust, and grow *your* relationship management skills by more accurately identifying **who** *you* are, **how** *you* communicate, and **why** *you* are inclined to relate, to manage, or to control *your* relationships in a particular way.

Circle the answers (on the following pages) to each question that most honestly apply to *you*. There are no <u>right</u> or <u>wrong</u> answers. At the end of each test, review *your* answers and then circle *your* honest assessment. (ex. Good / not so good)

9.1　How <u>friendly</u> are *You*?

1. How do you initiate friendship with a totally new person?

   a.　With a smile?

   b.　By introducing yourself?

   c.　By inviting to coffee? Lunch?

2. How easily do you connect with new people?

   a.　Very easily

   b.　Not easily

   c.　Barely, if ever

3. What do you do on weekends and holidays?

   a.　Spend time with friends

   b.　Spend time with family or alone

   c.　Play it by ear

4. What do you do at a good party or night club?

   a.　Meet new people

   b.　Stick with friends or familiar faces

   c.　Keep to yourself and people watch

5. What do your current friends say about you?

   a.　Outgoing, Extrovert

b. Pleasant to be around

c. Introverted, quiet

d. Not sure what they say

6. How many people in your neighborhood know you?

   a. All of them

   b. About half of them

   c. Very few of them

7. Are you comfortable inviting an acquaintance for coffee and a friendly chat?

   a. Very comfortable

   b. Depends on acquaintance

   c. Not very comfortable

8. Friendly / Not so friendly *(circle one)*

9.2 Are *you* a <u>good</u> friend?

1. Do you share a friend's secrets with others? Y/N

2. Do you wish friend(s) well on their birthdays? Y/N

3. Do you get into unnecessary arguments with your friend(s)? Y/N

4. Do you apologize for your mistakes? Y/N

5. If your friend is feeling badly, do you try to your cheer him/her up? Y/N

6. Are you courteous and polite with your friend(s)? Y/N

7. Do you pay compliments and offer congratulations easily? Y/N

8. Do you share material things easily with your friend(s)? Y/N

9. Do you allow friends to counsel or comfort you when they think that you need it? Y/N

10. Good friend / Not so good a friend *(circle one)*

9.3   How well do *you* <u>relate</u> to people?

1. If you see two people arguing, can you settle the argument? Y/N

2. Do you empathize with people who are different? Y/N

3. Is common courtesy important to you? Y/N

4. Do you smile/speak to people easily and are not offended if they do not reply? Y/N

5. Do you enjoy people watching? Y/N

6. Are your pets more important than your friend(s)? Y/N

7. Do you label/judge others easily? Y/N

8. Do you avoid responding to phone calls or emails? Y/N

9. Are you comfortable in crowds? Y/N

10. Do you engage strangers easily when out shopping? Y/N

11. Well / Not so well *(circle one)*

9.4 Do *you* <u>value</u> friendships?

1. Do you respond to a friend's email or phone call promptly? Y/N

2. Do you let your friends know how much you appreciate them? Y/N

3. Are you happy when your friend(s) finds success or happiness? Y/N

4. Are you there for your friends in a time of need? Y/N

5. Can you overlook the quirks and see your friend's heart? Y/N

6. Do you apologize when you have dissapointed a friend? Y/N

7. Do you remember your friend's birthdays and/or anniversaries? Y/N

8. Have you ever sent a friendship card? Y/N

9. Do you plan outtings with your friend(s)? Y/N

10. Based upon your responses above, <u>circle</u> the answer that best describes you:

    a. Very much   b. Not so much

9.5   The <u>chemistry</u> scale

For those relationships that have intimacy or romance as a component, it would be wise to proactively guage the level of chemistry; particularly if communication becomes labored or trust is broken. Below are some questions to ask of yourself.

1. I am no longer physically attracted to my partner. T/F

2. I feel that my partner is no longer physically attracted to me. T/F

3. I tell my partner frequently that I find him/her attractive. T/F

4. My partner tells me frequently that I am attractive. T/F

5. I still flirt with my partner. T/F

6. My partner still flirts me. T/F

7. My partner and I still kiss and carress frequently. T/F

8. Intimate moments with my partner are satisfying. T/F

9. I love to give my partner physical pleasure. T/F

10. My partner and I truly enjoy each others company. T/F

11. My partner often seeks alone time away from me. T/F

12. My partner takes my hand or holds me without prompting. T/F

13. I look forward to seeing my partner at the end of the day. T/F

14. MY partner doesn't seem to notice if I am not around. T/F

15. My partner compliments me in front of others. T/F

16. We have great chemistry / some chemistry / no chemistry *(circle one)*

Scoring

Add up the total number of answers that are True and the total number that are False. If your total number of Trues is atleast 10, your chemistry is very good. If your total number of Falses is 8 or more, your chemistry is minimal and a romantic renaissance may be in order.

9.6 The <u>rapport</u> test *'give it a try'*

What follows is a list of 41 **'A'** or **'B'** questions that can serve as a great conversation starter and as an initial insight into rapport. Make a copy of this list and share it with friends and acquaintances.

Try to get through all of the questions by not spending more than a few minutes on each. Find out how much *(simpatico)* or how little *(commonality)* you and your acquaintance or friend actually have in common.

There are no **right** or **wrong** answers; there are only predispositions and preferences.

1. Religious or spiritual?

2. Introverted or extroverted?

3. Leader or follower?

4. Ambitious or easy-going?

5. Cats or dogs?

6. Cake or Pie?

7. Onion rings or French fries?

8. Catsup or mustard?

9. Tartar sauce or cocktail sauce?

10. Beer or wine?

11. Coke or Pepsi?

12. Meats or vegetables?

13. Grill out or cook in?

14. Tea or coffee?

15. Water or soda?

16. Tennis or Golf?

17. Basketball or Football?

18. Spring or Fall?

19. Summer or Winter?

20. Morning person or night owl?

21. Breakfast or Dinner?

22. Cruise ship or Resort?

23. The mountains or the beach?

24. Watch movies or listen to music?

25. History Channel or Cartoon network?

26. Texting or calling?

27. Dancing or people watching?

28. Comedy or drama/suspense?

29. Action/adventure or love story?

30. Star wars or Star Trek?

31. Superman or Batman?

32. Liberal or conservative?

33. Small town or Big city?

34. Flirty or reserved?

35. Stylish or simple?

36. Holidays or birthdays?

37. Planes or Trains?

38. Car or SUV?

39. The Beatles or The Beach boys?

40. Thomas Jefferson or Abraham Lincoln?

41. Leonardo da Vinci or Michelangelo?

42. Cher or Madonna?

Note: This is meant to be a <u>fun</u> and <u>non-judgmental</u> tool for uncovering areas of common interest and to aid in sharing the 'authentic' *you*.

9.7   The <u>priority</u> checklist for partners

Your socio-economic status, *your* wants, *your* needs, and *your* priorities will change over the course of *your* life. Below is a list of relationship concerns that typically require some level of prioritization. Make two copies of this list. Give one to *your* prospective partner. Individually mark the number (1 less important, 5 most important) that best matches *your* level of priority; then, compare your respective choices.

Owning a home	1	2	3	4	5
Income	1	2	3	4	5
New car	1	2	3	4	5
Savings	1	2	3	4	5
Education	1	2	3	4	5
Having children	1	2	3	4	5
New clothes	1	2	3	4	5
Health care	1	2	3	4	5
Home improvement	1	2	3	4	5
Family	1	2	3	4	5
Travel	1	2	3	4	5
Entertainment	1	2	3	4	5
Debts	1	2	3	4	5
Pets	1	2	3	4	5
Sports	1	2	3	4	5

Charity	1	2	3	4	5
Fitness	1	2	3	4	5
Grooming	1	2	3	4	5
Sex	1	2	3	4	5
Holidays	1	2	3	4	4
Religion	1	2	3	4	5

This list can be a very effective tool in stimulating early constructive dialogue and in helping to determine if the level of compatibility desired for serious commitments exists.

9.8 The *'one minute'* <u>compatibility</u> test for romantic partners

1. Would *you* want to have a child with this person?

2. Would *you* want *your* child to grow up to be like this person?

3. Do *you* want to become more like this person?

4. Would *you* be willing to spend the rest of *your* life with this person if they remained just the way that *they* are right now?

<u>Results:</u>

- A yes to all <u>four</u> questions indicates <u>great</u> compatibility.

- A yes to <u>three</u> questions indicates <u>good</u> compatibility.

- A yes to <u>two</u> questions indicates <u>average</u> compatibility.

- A yes to only <u>one</u> question indicates <u>poor</u> compatibility.

- A no to <u>all</u> questions indicates <u>no</u> meaningful compatibility.

9.9   Relationship 'profiling'

On the next page are (13) opportunities to profile your various relationship partners. Fill in as many as you feel confident in completing by using the **who** (social style/introvert/extrovert), the **how** (control drama/rapport type), and the **why** (attachment style, history) descriptions of each found in the previous sections.

Dominant social style: (section 2.3)

- Driver (Dr)
- Analytical (An)

- Amiable (Am)
- Expressive (Ex)

Dominant rapport type: (section 3.3)

- Auditory (A)
- Visual (V)

- Kinesthetic (K)
- Balanced (AVK)

Dominant control drama: (section 6.7)

- Intimidator (Intim)
- Interrogator (Inter)

- Aloof (Al)
- Poor me (Pm)

Dominant attachment style: (section 3.6)

- Secure (Sec)
- Anxious (Anx)

- Avoidant (Av)
- Ambivalent (Amb)

Using the descriptions on the previous page, write the dominant (only) codes beneath the 5 categories below that best match the <u>observed</u> profile of each of *your* respective relationship partners.

Profile factors:	Social style	(I)ntrovert (E)xtrovert	Rapport type	Control drama	Attachment style
Codes:	Am, Ex, Dr, An	Intro / Extro	V, A, K	Inter, Intim, PM, Al	Sec, Anx, Avo, Amb
1. You *					
2. Sister					
3. Brother					
4. Wife					
5. Husband					
6. Female friend					
7. Male friend					
8. Co-worker					
9. Boss					
10. Room-mate					
11. child					
12. Mother					
13. Father					

Which relationships have been the <u>most</u> difficult? # ___, ___, ___, ___

Which relationships have been the <u>least</u> difficult? # ___, ___, ___, ___

Anonymous

The final step: 'Sharing' this approach

<u>Defintion:</u> using or enjoying something jointly with others

"Friendship is a precious force that has no parallel; there is no other single human power that can generate good qualities in a person as a true friendship".

Robert E. Hall

After a certain age, children stop emulating *their* parents and start imitating *their* friends. For this reason, *our* **friending** skills sets - initiated for most of *us* in pre-school - must continually evolve.

We began FRIENDSFIRST by following *our* friends <u>You</u> and <u>Me</u> as the bears discovered the three relationship **conditions** (section 1.1), the three levels of **involvement** (section 1.4) within those conditions, and the three levels of **affection** (section 1.5). We agreed that those who enjoy the best and longest lasting relationships of *any* condition had established a real friendship first.

Next, *we* discussed *your* **P**ersonal **O**perating **S**ystem (section 2.1), *your* **brands** (section 2.2), *your* **social style** (section 2.4) and **temperament** (section 2.8), *your* **truth** (section 3.1), the importance of **rapport** (section 3.2), **introverts** vs **extroverts**,

relational competence (section 3.5) and **attachment styles** (section 3.6) to determine *your* current message and the various ways that *you* might better communicate the 'authentic' you to both acquaintances and friends.

After developing an understanding of **acquaintances** (section 4.1), **friending** (section 4.4), your **emotional bank account** (section 4.6) and the **relationship cycle** (section 5.1), we revisited your **P. O. S.** (section 6.1) again to: uncover your **must haves**, discuss **paradigm shifts** (section 6.3), understand the affects of **Neuro-Associative Conditioning** (section 6.4), highlight the importance of **emotional intelligence** (section 6.5) and stress the importance of avoiding **control dramas** (section 6.7).

The caveat? Do not fall into the trap of making exceptions to *your* **P. O. S.** because of a heightened sense of rapport or because of a strong physical attraction.

The **pursuers** and the **pursued** (section 7.0) offered advice on how best to deal with an imbalance in rapport, social style, and/or attraction and the discomfort that can be experienced when interests are not mutual or reciprocated.

Finally; *your* part in the success of any relationship condition involving family, co-workers, or social friends will rest entirely upon *your* abilities to **profile** others properly and to honor the **relationship pact** (section 8.1); the ten rules of the pact will: help keep *you* from sabotaging *your* happiness, help *you* to make better relationship choices, and help *you* to be a better friend to others.

According to motivational speaker Tom Hopkins, a person must be exposed to new material six times before he or she is able to retain 62 percent of what they have learned. Read FRIENDS FIRST again and then discuss its contents with family, friend(s) or partner(s). Ask for *their* sincere and constructive observations of *your* respective relationships and offer the same positive feedback. Be willing to make positive changes to *your* friending habits and be willing to reconcile *your* various <u>relationship conditions</u> (section 1.0) in a sincere effort to help **better** those relationships.

Some immediate suggestions. If *you* don't already do so, try engaging acquaintances with more than a <u>brief</u> smile or a <u>passing</u> hello. Consider sharing the fellowship of *your* existing friends and companions with *new* aquaintances. Roger & Sally Horchow - in their book *'The Art of Friendship'* - remind *us* that there is no substitute for real and meaningful human interaction. Ask an acquaintance or a friend to join *you* for coffee or lunch and show a genuine interest in *their* day. Call an old friend or a family member today and remind *them* that *you* care. Start planting good friending seeds in new, as well as, familiar places and watch *your* relationship garden grow.

If *you* - initially - believed that the healthiest and the longest lasting relationships are between the best of friends, it is my sincere hope that FRIENDS FIRST has offered *you* a deeper insight into the all-important and universal <u>components</u> of relationships and, thus, proven *your* intuiton to be correct.

"Want <u>better</u> relationships? Become a <u>better</u> friend!"

友谊

"Don't spend time beating on a wall hoping to transform it into a door."

Dr. Laura Schlessinger

Useful <u>terms</u> & <u>phrases</u>: within the context of relationships

Affable – good-natured; courteous

Affectation - artificial manner of behavior

Affinity - liking or attraction; feeling of kinship

Akin - related by blood; similar

Amenable – responsive; accountable

Amiable – good-natured; friendly

Amicable – friendly; peaceable

Argumentative - inclined to argue

'Attention junkies' – (subjective) those in constant need of acknowledgement, validation or interaction with others with little regard for the outcome

'Authentic power' – (subjective) strength that is internal and is not exerted upon others; the power to give, inspire, and create

Belligerent - hostile; confrontational

126

Besotted - *infatuated*

Catharsis - *a release of emotional tensions through an experience that allows pent-up feelings to flow freely*

'Co-dependents' - *two people who share a mutual need for attention, help, or support*

Condescend – *to patronize; to feign equality or empathy*

Courting - *the attention paid to a person to gain favor or affection*

'Deal breakers' - *(subjective) circumstances, events, habits or changes that void initial agreements or understandings*

Deprecate – *to express disapproval of*

Desist – *to cease; to abstain*

Devolve - *to pass personal responsibilty or duties on to someone else*

Disingenuous - *insincere; not candid*

'Double lives' - *(subjective) non-primary relationships lead in secrecy and in contradiction with the public persona*

'Emotional bank account' - *a metaphor describing the amount of trust accrued in a relationship.*

'Emotional divorce' - *(subjective) an emotional disconnect from a relationship partner that is seldom punitive but does tend to disrupt communication*

'Emotional integrity' - *(subjective) owning and sharing feelings and emotions as they occur without filters*

Empathy - *the capacity to identify with a person and/or circumstance*

Entrust - *to give something into the care of another*

Equanimity - composure; evenness in temperment

'Extremists' - (subjective) those consistently inclined to exxaggerate matters and who use terms like all, always, and never

'False advertising' - (subjective) presenting information or impressions that are not authentic or true to gain favor

Feminine - characteristic of women

'Filtering' - (subjective) selectively dispensing or sharing information based on self-serving needs or fears

'Fixer upper' - (subjective) persons percieved as viable relationship partners given a sizeable investment of time and effort and change

Habit - a regular tendency or practice that serves some purpose

'History buffs' - (subjective) those who specialize in reliving past hurts or slights to justify their unyeilding actions or attitudes

'Honey mooners' - (subjective) those who enjoy the initial phases of an initimate or romantic relationship but who have no skills, plans or confidence in long term involvements

Insecure - subject to fears or doubts; not self-confident or assured; anxious

Jaunty - cheerful and self-confident

Je ne sais quoi - (fr) a typically positive quality that defies a cmplete definition or an adequate description

Jealousy - a state of fear, suspicion, or envy caused by a real or imagined threat or challenge to one's possesive instincts

Joie de vivre - (fr) exhibiting exuberance; high spirits; a joy of life

'Living outloud' - (subjective) fully embracing your brand(s), your culture, your beliefs, your fears, and your voice in an appropriately public way

Love lorn - pining from unreciprocated love

'Martyrs' - (subjective) a person who needs to be seen and identified as making great sacrifices for their relationship

Masculine - relating to or characteristic of men

Metta - (buddhist) loving kindness; the nature of a friend

Mollify - to appease

Passion - strong emotion or enthusiasm

Passive - not inclined to show initiative; inclined to be reactive

'Personal honesty' - (subjective) a deliberate and continuous attempt to uncover and express your genuine and personal truths

Project - to cause (oneself) to enter/infer imaginatively

Puffery - exaggerated flattery or praise of self or others

Quibbling - engaging in chatter that is argumentative, unproductive, disingenuous and discourteous

'Rationing' - (subjective) an intentional effort to control the affection and communication shared with others as a form of relational leveraging

'Relationship cycle' - (subjective) the movement of relationships through phases of positive and/or negative evolutions

Sanguine - optimistic; confident

Sagacious - keen and perceptive

Simpatico - Of like mind or temperament; compatible; having attractive qualities; pleasing; gets along well; congenial

Smitten - aroused by an intense emotion

'Soul mate' – (subjective) a person 'ideally' suited to another

Synergy - partners working together to produce an effect greater than the sum of their individual efforts

Tryst - a secret meeting of lovers

Ultimatum - a demand in negotiations; if not accepted or agreed upon, infers loss, or punishment

'Unrequited love' – love that is not openly expressed or reciprocated

Vain - having too high an opinion of one's looks or abilities

Venerable - entitled to respect on account of character

Veracious - truthful

Visceral - of feelings rather than reason

'Walk your talk' - (subjective) turning verbalized intentions into obeservable actions

友谊

'Trouble' shooting: strategies and suggestions

Score relationship points right <u>now</u>!

the top eleven suggestions

- Offer an unsolicited hug.

- Let someone know that <u>their</u> happiness matters to you.

- Stand or sit still and just listen.

- Find a way to make your friend or acquaintance laugh.

- Offer to pick up a favorite food, beverage, or dessert.

- Pay an unexpected and meaningful compliment.

- Make a spontaneous invitation to a movie or concert tonight.

- Send a 'thinking of you' greeting card.

- Routinely have friends relay timely and thoughtful messages of affection to other friends .

- Write a handwritten note or letter expressing feelings of appreciation and support.

- Find the time to take some spontaneous and playful pictures together.

- Plan a fun occasion to get 'dressed up' or 'dressed down'.

- Show a greater interest in the welfare of your family, your friends and your co-workers right now.

Breakthrough *don't* **breakdown:**

The 6 rules of communication for the speaker and the listener

The speaker:

- Be brief and be specific.

- Do not insult, blame or accuse your friend.

- Do not use threats, absolutes or labels.

- State your concerns positively.

- Do not draw your own conclusions prematurely.

- Use "I feel" instead of "you don't". Avoid fault finding.

The listener:

- Listen attentively and strive to maintain 'positive' eye contact.

- Do not be defensive or counterattack; no quibbling!

- If asked, clarify the reasons for your behavior; but, do not argue or make excuses.

- Do not analyze your friend's motives.

- Summarize aloud and respectfully what you think your friend means.

- Apologize immediately and sincerely when you have hurt or upset your friend.

'Reconciling' romance or intimacy back to platonic: *eight suggestions*

- Take a break from all communication for a minimum of one week to avoid <u>control dramas</u>.

- Keep it <u>platonic</u>! Once communication does resume, avoid arguments, and romantic or intimate subjects.

- Know your <u>limits</u>. Do not engage in conversations or allow contact that makes you uncomfortable.

- Do not relive the past. Mutually agree to a fresh start as <u>platonic</u> friends.

- Do not be begged, bullied, or cajoled into continuing the <u>romance</u> or the <u>intimacy</u>. Again! Avoid <u>control dramas</u>!

- Avoid any attempts at 'quick fixes'; especially the physical/intimate kind. Just say no!

- Fill the companionship void by spending more time with family, other friends, or co-workers.

- If your sincere attempts at <u>reconciling</u> do not work, be emotionally prepared and resolved to <u>retire</u> the relationship.

Bad relationship 'fixes': *7 suggestions 'back to good'*

- Use the 'breakthrough, don't break down' approach.

- Determine <u>together</u> what the problems are and write them down. No 'mind' reading or 'projecting' allowed!

- <u>Accept</u> and clearly <u>express</u> responsibility for <u>your</u> part in the breakdown.

- Revisit each others <u>early</u> expectations to see if they were <u>clear</u> and were <u>understood</u>.

- Adopt new/revised relationship rules. <u>Talk</u> them out. <u>Write</u> them down. <u>Post</u> them up.

- <u>Forgive</u> and <u>reconnect</u>. Put the new rules and new attitudes into action. Avoid perceptions of indifference or aloofness.

- Avoid using <u>ultimatums</u> or <u>threats</u> to achieve goals no matter how subtle the wording or the actions.

"Forgiveness is giving up the hope that the past could have been any different."

Anonymous

Relationship 'pitfalls' to avoid: the top 8 'oopses'

- Avoid getting too attached too soon. Don't get ahead of your 'friendship'.

- Avoid expecting one person to 'complete' you.

- Do not sacrifice established and valued friendships in order to mollify the fears or to appease the demands of a new one.

- Avoid trying to 'control' your partner. This only reveals your fears, your insecurities and your inflexibility.

- Avoid playing the 'blame' game. Share in the successes and the failures or your relationship. Accept your role.

- Avoid quibbling, beligerence and rudeness. Respect and civility are paramount to a 'healthy' relationship.

- Do not use threats, initimidation, or ultimatums. Ever!

- Avoid comparisons with others. They are never objective, appreciated, or fair.

Getting past <u>rejection</u> or <u>loss</u>: *"we all experience it"*

- Remind yourself daily that any pain or sense of loss will eventually end. Write your thoughts and feelings down in a daily journal.

- It's ok to be dissapointed but not devastated. Express your hurt without antagonizing or imposing.

- Take the opportunity to look at your feelings honestly, to learn from them humbly, and to move forward confidently.

- Turn a negative relationship 'what if?' into a positive 'what next?' Make amends. Forgive yourself and your partner.

- Lean positively on the friendship and the support of others.

- Seek counseling if the pain and/or sense of loss seem inescapable.

- Accept yourself. Respect yourself. Trust yourself. Love yourself. Stretch yourself.

Relationship 'retirement' suggestions:

'7 steps to moving on'

- Be absolutely sure that you <u>want</u> and are <u>ready</u> for the relationship to end.

- If possible, address the problem(s) using the 'breakthrough' method on page 133.

- Apologize sincerely for any mistakes and/or misunderstandings.

- State clearly your intentions and your resolve to discontinue the relationship.

- Share the positives; avoid the negatives. Be mature and avoid hurtful words.

- State any new rules clearly: (ex) limited calls, no visits, no emails, limited texts, ect. (agree amicably)

- Stand your ground. Avoid 'feeling' words. Do not give in to emotion or fear!

友谊

Friendship quotes: *timeless words of wisdom*

"Old friends pass away, new friends appear. It is just like the days. An old day passes, a new day arrives. The important thing is to make it meaningful: a meaningful friend - or a meaningful day.

Dalai Lama

"It is better to be to be in chains with friends than to be in a garden with strangers."

Persian proverb

"A real friend walks in when the rest of the world walks out."

Anonymous

"A friend will continue to believe in you when you have ceased to believe in yourself."

Anonymous

"The better part of one's life consists of his friendships."
Abraham Lincoln

"Sometimes you pick your friends. Sometimes they pick you."
Anonymous

"Friendship with oneself is all-important because without it one cannot be friends with anyone else in the world."
Eleanor Roosevelt

"Misfortune reveals those who are not true friends."
Aristotle

"What is a friend? A single soul in two bodies."
Aristotle

"My best friend is the one who brings out the best in me."
Aristotle

"The making of friends, who are real friends, is the best token we have of a man's success in life."
Edward Hale

"Friendship without self interest is one of the rare and beautiful things in life."

James F. Byrnes

"If you have more than one friend, consider yourself rich."
Anonymous

"True friendship is the highest form of love."

Anonymous

"True friends can sit in complete silence and have the most wonderful time."

Anonymous

"The only reward of virtue is virtue; the only way to have a friend is to be one."

Ralph Waldo Emerson

"Too late, we learn, a man must hold his friend un-judged, accepted, ...trusted to the end."

John Boyle O'reilly

"Walking with a friend in the dark is better than walking alone in the light."

Helen Keller

"I get by with a little help from my friends."

Joe Cocker

"Fate chooses your relations; you choose your friends."

Jacques Delille

"Remember that every good friend was once a stranger."

Anonymous

"That which is striking and beautiful is not always good, but that which is good is always beautiful."
                    Anonymous

"The best things in life aren't things."
                    Art Buchwald

"Truth fears no questions but questions some fears."
                    Robert E. Hall

"Every time we open our mouths, men look into our minds."
                    Anonymous

"Better to do something imperfectly than nothing flawlessly."
                    Robert Schuller

"Experience is not what happens to a man; it is what a man   does with what happens to him."
                    Aldous Huxley

"Live dangerously; take risks; cultivate eccentricity, which means growing closer to being yourself. This will give you a life worth living and of which you can be proud."
                    Thomas D. Willhite

"friendship multiplies the good of life and divides the evil."
                    Baltasar Gracian

"the ideal friendship is to feel as one while remaining two."
                    Anne S. Swetchine

"Often, we will make more time for our enemies than we do for our friends."

Anonymous

"Don't walk in front of me, I may not follow; Don't walk behind me, I may not lead; Just walk beside me and be my friend."

Albert Carnus

"Where there are friends, there is wealth."

Titus Maccius Plautus

"We don't see things as they are; we see them as we are."

Anais Nin

"Not half, but man's entire life is established on friendship, companionship, and an association with the good."

Buddha

"The best mirror is an old friend."

George Herbert

"Everything that irritates us about others can lead us to an understanding of ourselves."

Carl Jung

"Pick battles big enough to matter, small enough to win."

Jonathan Kozol

"Only the curious will learn and only the resolute will overcome the obstacles to learning."

Eugene S. Wilson

"Every person is the creation of himself, the image of his own thinking and believing. As individuals think and believe, so they are."

Claude M. Bristol

"A true friend never gets in your way unless you happen to be going down."

Arnold Glasow

"The most beautiful discovery true friends make is that they can grow separately without growing apart."

Elisabeth Foley

"Remember, happiness doesn't depend upon who you are or what you have; it depends solely upon what you think."

Dale Carnegie

"The antidote for fifty enemies is one friend."

Aristotle

"True friendship comes when silence between two people is comfortable."

Dave Tyson Gentry

"If a man does not make new acquaintances as he advances through life, he will soon find himself alone. A man should keep his friendships in constant repair."

Samuel Johnson

"The best kind of friend is the one you could sit on a porch with, never saying a word, and walk away feeling like that was the best conversation you've had."

Author Unknown

"The language of friendship is not words but meanings."

Henry David Thoreau

"Cherish the friend who tells you a harsh truth, wanting ten times more to tell you a loving lie."

Robert Brault

"It is not so much our friends' help that helps us, as the confidence of their help."

Epicurus

"Nothing but heaven itself is better than a friend who is really a friend."

Plautus

"The best time to make friends is before you need them."

Ethel Barrymore

"A friend can tell you things you don't want to tell yourself."

Frances Ward Weller

"A friend accepts us as we are yet helps us to be what we should."

Author unknown

"Anyone can become angry - that is easy. But to be angry with the right person, to the right degree, at the right time, for the right purpose, and in the right way - this is not easy."

Aristotle

"the road to a friend's house is never too long."

Danish Proverb

"If all of my friends were to jump off a bridge, I wouldn't jump with them; I'd be at the bottom to catch them."

Author unknown

"A friend drops their plans when you're in trouble, shares joy in your accomplishments, and feels sad when you're in pain. A friend encourages your dreams and offers advice...but when you don't follow it, they still respect and love you."

Doris Wild Helmering

"Our friends don't see our faults, or conceal them, or soften them."

Joseph Addison

"No love, no friendship can cross the path of our destiny without leaving some mark on it forever."

Francois Mauriac

"Since there is nothing so well worth having as friends, never lose a chance to make them."

Francesco Guicciardini

"'Tis a great confidence in a friend to tell him your faults; greater to tell him his."

Benjamin Franklin

"With every good-bye, we must also be willing and able to let go."

Robert E. Hall

"If you want to go fast, go alone; if you want to go far, go together."

African proverb

"A friend is one to whom one may pour out all the contents of one's heart - chaff and grain together - knowing that the gentlest of hands will take it and sift it, keep what is worth keeping and with a breath of kindness blow the rest away."

Arabian proverb

"Without trust, those who would be friends remain only acquaintances."

Robert E. Hall

"Friends are God's way of taking care of us."

Anonymous

"Without friends, no one would choose to live, though he had all other goods."

Aristotle

"We neither deserve all of our enemies nor all of our friends."

Robert E. Hall

"A friend sees the first tear, catches the second, and stops the third."

Anonymous

"Happiness comes of the capacity to feel deeply, to enjoy simply, to think freely, to risk life,...to be needed."

Storm Jameson

"Integrity begins by telling self the truth. Honesty is practiced by telling the truth to others."

Robert E. Hall

"Every time we open our mouths, men look into our minds."

Anonymous

References:

Personal Styles & Effective performance

    David W. Merrill, Ph.D. and Roger H. Reid, M.A.

Life strategies

    Phillip C. McGraw, Ph.D.

Relationship Rescue

    Phillip C. McGraw, Ph.D.

Personal freedom

    Gerry Spence

The Psychologist's book of personality tests

    Louis Janda, Ph.D.

Ten stupid things that men do to mess up their lives

    Dr. Laura Schlessinger

Ten stupid things women do to mess up their lives

    Dr. Laura Schlessinger

Survival skills for the modern man

    Donn M. Davis

First things first

    Stephen R. Covey, A. Roger Merrill, Rebecca Merrill

UCLA study on friendship among women

    Gale Berkowitz 2002

What are friends for? A longer life

    Tara Parker-Pope / NY Times

Instant Rapport

    Michael Brooks

Social competence

    M.B. Gurtman

The 7 habits of highly effective people

    Steven R. Covey

Men are from Mars, women are from Venus

    John Gray, Ph.D.

The art of mingling

    Jeanne Martinet

Practical Intuition

    Laura Day

Life's greatest lessons

    Hal Urban

The power of intention

    Dr. Wayne W. Dyer

Ten talks about sex and character

    Pepper Schwartz, Ph.D.

Sexual intelligence

    Dr. Sheree Conrad & Dr. Michael Milburn

The how of happiness

    Sonja Lyubomirsky

The Good marriage

    Judith S. Wallerstein & Sandra Blakeslee

Sex in human loving

      Eric Berne M.D.

Love Cycles, the science of intimacy

      Winnifred B. Cutler, Ph.D.

Lies at the altar

      Dr. Robin L. Smith

Love is never enough

      Aaron T. Beck, M.D.

He's just not that in to you

      Greg Behrendt and Liz Tuccillo

The Conversation

      Hill Harper

His needs Her needs

      Dr. Willard F. Harley, Jr.

Life 101

      John-Roger and Peter McWilliams

He-Motions

    T. D. Jakes

The Art of Friendship

    Roger Horchow & Sally Horchow

10 Bad Choices That Ruin Black Women's Lives

    Dr. Grace Cornish Livingstone, Ph.D. M.P.S.

Awaken the giant within

    Anthony Robbins

Unlimited Power

    Anthony Robbins

Dateable: are you? are they?

    Justin Lookadoo and Hayley Morgan

Turn ons; pleasing yourself while you please your lover

    Lonnie Barbach, Ph.D.

The hard questions: 100 essential questions to ask before you say "I do!"

    Susan Piver

Getting through to people

    Jesse S. Nirenberg, Ph.D.

Emotional Intelligence: Why it can matter more than IQ

    Daniel Goleman, Ph.D.

Don't sweat the small stuff in love

    Richard Carlson, Ph.D. and Kristine Carlson

Why can't I fall in love: a 12 step program

    Shmuley Boteach

A new look at Love

    Elaine Walster and G. William Walster

The Price of Love

    Tanisha Bagley

The Celestine Prophecy

    James Redfield

How to make people like you in 90 seconds or less

    Nicholas Boothman

Single No More, how and where to meet your perfect mate

    Ellen Kreidman, Ph.D.

Are you the one for me?

    Barbara De Angelis, Ph.D.

Love between equals

    Pepper Schwartz, Ph.D.

Desirable Men, how to find them

    Nancy Fagan

The five love languages

    Gary Chapman

Character & Temperament Types

    David Keirsey and Marilyn Bates

I never knew I had a choice

    Gerald Corey, Marianne Schneider Corey

Perspectives on Personality

    Carver Scheier

Resources:

Toll free helplines:

U.S. Department of Health and Human Services (HHS)

Substance abuse and mental health services administration (SAMHSA)

1-800-662-HELP (4357)

National Domestic Violence hotline

24 hour crisis assistance; shelters, legal advocacy, health care centers, and counseling

1-800-799-SAFE (7233)

Psychologist (local referral)

1-800-964-2000

Sexually transmitted disease

1-800-227-8922

Pregnancy (24 hours)

1-800-238-4269

Local resources: Mental Health crisis hotline in your local phone book's government pages

Relationship related websites:

www.aamft.org

www.relationship-rescue.net

www.lifescript.com

www.mentalhelp.net

www.relationship-help.com

www.sexualhealth.com

www.relationshipspecialist.com

www.wholefamily.com

About the author

Screenwriter (Writers guild of America, East), author, architectural designer, broadcast veteran, entrepreneur, member of Toastmasters International, and the US Army - Corps of Engineers, Robert Hall has turned his unique collective of educational, professional, military, and life experiences - as well as his extensive self-study on the 'human renaissance' - into a thought-provoking dialogue on relationships.

Mr. Hall has been a featured guest on the TV show *'Getting to the source with Clovia'*, as well as the Radio program *'Real talk for real men - Community conversations with Clovia Lawrence';* In addition, Mr. Hall has been featured as the guest speaker on relationships during the 3rd annual Men's Forum: *'Listen up ladies, men are talking'* held June 26, 2010 in Richmond, Virginia.

Mr. Hall grew up in the suburbs of Washington, DC and currently resides in Richmond, Virginia.

友谊

Notes

友谊

Notes

友谊

Notes

友谊

Notes